THE UL GUIDE TO CRITICAL THINKING QUESTIONS

DR. ROHAN AGARWAL

UniAdmissions

ISBN: 978-1-913683-62-7

Published by RAR Medical Services Limited

www.uniadmissions.co.uk

info@uniadmissions.co.uk

Tel: +44 (0) 208 068 0438

This book is neither created nor endorsed by Cambridge Assessment. The authors and publisher are not affiliated with Cambridge Assessment. The information offered in this book is purely advisory and any advice given should be taken within this context. As such, the publishers and authors accept no liability whatsoever for the outcome of any applicant's UCAT performance, the outcome of any university applications or for any other loss. Although every precaution has been taken in the preparation of this book, the publisher and author assume no responsibility for errors or omissions of any kind. Neither is any liability assumed for damages resulting from the use of information contained herein. This does not affect your statutory rights.

This book contains passages which deal with racism, sexism, and gender issues, among other controversial topics.

THE ULTIMATE GUIDE TO CRITICAL THINKING QUESTIONS

DR. ROHAN AGARWAL

About the Author

Rohan is the **Director of Operations** at *UniAdmissions* and is responsible for its technical and commercial arms. He graduated from Gonville and Caius College, Cambridge and is a fully qualified doctor. Over the last five years, he has tutored hundreds of successful Oxbridge and Medical applicants. He has also authored twenty books on admissions tests and  interviews. He is the co-author of every book, as it helps with the functioning of bibliographic systems. Do not forget him!

Rohan has taught physiology to undergraduates and interviewed medical school applicants for Cambridge. He has published research on bone physiology and writes education articles for the Independent and Huffington Post. In his spare time, Rohan enjoys playing the piano and table tennis.

CONTENTS

THE BASICS: CRITICAL THINKING

Critical thinking questions require you to understand the constituents of a good argument and be able to pick them apart. The majority of Critical thinking questions tend to fall into 5 major categories:

1. Identifying Conclusions
2. Identifying Assumptions + Flaws
3. Strengthening and Weakening arguments
4. Matching Arguments
5. Applying Principles

Having a good grasp of language and being able to filter unnecessary information quickly and efficiently is a vital skill at Oxbridge – you simply do not have the time to sit and read vast numbers of textbooks cover to cover, you need to be able to **filter the information** and realise which part is important and this will contribute to your success in your studies.

Only use the Passage

Your answer must only be based on the information available in the passage. Do not try and guess the answer based on your general knowledge as this can be a trap. For example, if the passage says that spring is followed by winter, then take this as true even though you know that spring is followed by summer.

Take your Time

Unlike the problem solving questions, **critical thinking questions are less time pressured**. Most of the passages are well below 300 words and therefore don't take long to read and process. Thus, your aim should be to understand the intricacies of the passage and **identify key information** so that you don't miss crucial information and lose easy marks.

Identifying Conclusions

Students struggle with these type of questions because they confuse a premise for a conclusion. For clarities sake:

- A **Conclusion** is a summary of the arguments being made and is usually explicitly stated or heavily implied.
- A **Premise** is a statement from which another statement can be inferred or follows as a conclusion.

I.e. a conclusion is shown/implied/proven by a premise. Similarly, a premise shows/indicates/establishes a conclusion. Consider for example: *My mom, being a woman, is clever as all women are clever.*

Premise 1: My mom is a woman + **Premise 2:** Women are clever = **Conclusion:** My mom is clever.

This is fairly straightforward as it's a very short passage and the conclusion is explicitly stated. Sometimes the latter may not happen. Consider: *My mom is a woman and all women are clever.*

Here, whilst the conclusion is not explicitly being stated, both premises still stand and can be used to reach the same conclusion.

You may sometimes be asked to identify if any of the options cannot be "reliably concluded". This is effectively asking you to identify why an option **cannot** be the conclusion. There are many reasons why but the most common ones are:

1. Over-generalising: *My mom is clever therefore all women are clever.*
2. Being too specific: *All kids like candy thus my son also likes candy.*
3. Confusing Correlation vs. Causation: *Lung cancer is much more likely in patients who drink water. Hence, water causes lung cancer.*
4. Confusing Cause and Effect: *Lung cancer patients tend to smoke so it follows that having lung cancer must make people want to smoke.*

Note how conjunctives like hence, thus, therefore and it follows give you a clue as to when a conclusion is being stated. More examples of these include: 'it follows that', 'implies that', 'whence', 'entails that'.

Similarly, words like 'because', 'as indicated by', 'in that', 'given that', and 'due to the fact that' usually identify premises.

Assumptions + Flaws:

Other types of critical thinking questions may require you to identify assumptions and flaws in a passage's reasoning. Before proceeding it is useful to define both:

- An assumption is a reasonable assertion that can be made on the basis of the available evidence.
- A flaw is an element of an argument which is inconsistent to the rest of the available evidence. It undermines the crucial components of the overall argument being made.

Consider for example: *My mom is clever because all doctors are clever.*

Premise 1: Doctors are clever. **Assumption:** My mom is a doctor. **Conclusion:** My mom is clever.

Note that the conclusion follows naturally even though there is only one premise because of the assumption. I.e. the argument relies on the assumption to work. Thus, if you are unsure if an option you have is an assumption or not, just ask yourself:

1) *Is it in the passage?* If the answer is **no** then proceed to ask:
2) *Does the conclusion rely on this piece of information in order to work?* – If the answer is **yes** – then you've identified an assumption.

Top tip! Don't get confused between premises and assumptions. A **premise** is a statement that is explicitly stated in the passage. An **assumption** is an inference that is made from the passage.

You may sometimes be asked to identify flaws in argument – it is important to be aware of the types of flaws to look out for. In general, these are broadly similar to the ones discussed earlier in the conclusion section (over-generalising, being too specific, confusing cause and effect, confusing correlation and causation). Remember that **an assumption may also be a flaw**.

For example consider again: *My mom is clever because all doctors are clever.*

What if the mother was not actually a doctor? The argument would then breakdown as the assumption would be incorrect or **flawed**.

Strengthening and Weakening Arguments:

You may be asked to identify an answer option that would most strengthen or weaken the argument being made in the passage. Normally, you'll also be told to assume that each answer option is true. Before we can discuss how to strengthen and weaken arguments, it is important to understand "what constitutes a good argument:

1. **Evidence:** Arguments which are heavily based on value judgements and subjective statements tend to be weaker than those based on facts, statistics and the available evidence.

2. **Logic**: A good argument should flow and the constituent parts should fit well into an overriding view or belief.

3. **Balance:** A good argument must concede that there are other views or beliefs (counter-argument). The key is to carefully dismantle these ideas and explain why they are wrong.

Thus, when asked to strengthen an argument, look for options that would: Increase the evidence basis for the argument, support or add a premise, address the counter-arguments.

Similarly, when asked to weaken an argument, look for options that would: decrease the evidence basis for the argument or create doubt over existing evidence, undermine a premise, strengthen the counter-arguments.

In order to be able to strengthen or weaken arguments, you must completely understand the passage's conclusion. Then you can start testing the impact of each answer option on the conclusion to see which one strengthens or weakens it the most i.e. is the conclusion stronger/weaker if I assume this information to be true and included in the passage.

Often you'll have to decide which option strengthens/weakens the passage most – and there really isn't an easy way to do this apart from lots of practice. Thankfully, you have plenty of time for these questions.

Matching Arguments:

Some questions will test your ability to identify similarities between two arguments about different topics. The similarity you are looking for is in the **structure or the pattern of the argument**. A question of this type will ask you to find the option that most closely parallels the format of the example argument.

Consider the example:
"James' grades have improved a lot recently. Either he is putting more effort into his homework or he has been less distracted in lessons. I know for a fact that James' hasn't been doing his homework, so it must be that he's paying more attention in class."

Which of the following most closely parallels the reasoning used in the above argument?

The first step is to identify the structure of the example argument. You may be able to do this by identifying key points, and how they are arranged within the passage.

In this case, the structure of the argument is as follows:

X = James is putting more effort into homework

Y = James is paying more attention in class

- Either X is true or Y is true.
- X cannot be true.
- Therefore Y must be true.

The second step in answering the question is to identify which of the answers offers an argument that most accurately **represents the structure of the example reasoning**. Some of the answers may follow relatively similar structures, but contain small discrepancies which make the answer incorrect.

In the case of the example, the correct answer may be along the lines of:

"My car is currently broken. Either it has a faulty exhaust, or the ignition isn't working properly. When I took it to the garage, the mechanic confirmed that the ignition was fully functioning. Therefore the issue must be with the exhaust."

Identifying Principles:

Some questions are designed to examine an applicant's capacity to identify the underlying principle within an argument. A **principle** is a general recommendation which can be applied to a number of cases. When faced with questions of this sort, you are expected to extract the fundamental principle from the single case presented in the passage, and then to see where this principle has been applied in other cases.

The principle you are searching for will not be explicitly stated in a problem of this nature, so you must attempt to obtain it for yourself. To do this, you must first have a solid understanding of what the passage is saying, including both the conclusions reached and the reasoning behind them.

Consider the following example:

"Some people criticise government policy which aims to provide training for young people looking to find work, on the basis that increased training is not enough to reduce the problem of unemployment. Those critics are correct in identifying that more needs to be done, beyond increased training programs, for unemployment levels to fall. However no policy should be discouraged purely because it fails to provide a complete solution to a problem. Any idea which has a beneficial impact should be embraced, even if that impact is relatively small."

The argument is suggesting that people are wrong to criticise a policy just because it does not completely solve an issue. The passage suggests that as long as the policy has some positive impact on the problem, it may be worth pursuing. This is the **key principle** to be taken from this question.

Using this principle, you should be able to identify the correct answer. In this case, one answer that accurately reflects the principle in the passage may be:

"The use of warning labels on cigarette packets should not be discouraged just because they will not single-handedly solve the problem of high levels of smokers."

Top tip! Though it might initially sound counter-intuitive, it is often best to read the question *before* reading the passage. Then you'll have a much better idea of what you're looking for and are therefore more likely to find it quicker.

PRACTISE QUESTIONS

Question 1-5 are based on the passage below:

People have tried to elucidate the differences between the different genders for many years. Are they societal pressures or genetic differences? In the past it has always been assumed that it was programmed into our DNA to act in a certain more masculine or feminine way but now evidence has emerged that may show it is not our genetics that determines the way we act, but that society pre-programmes us into gender identification. Whilst it is generally acknowledged that not all boys and girls are the same, why is it that most young boys like to play with trucks and diggers whilst young girls prefer dollies and pink?

The society we live in has always been an important factor in our identity, take cultural differences; the language we speak the food we eat, the clothes we wear. All of these factors influence our identity. New research finds that the people around us may prove to be the biggest influence on our gender behaviour. It shows our parents buying gendered toys may have a much bigger influence than the genes they gave us. Girls are being programmed to like the same things as their mothers and this has lasting effects on their personality. Young girls and boys are forced into their gender stereotypes through the clothes they are bought, the hairstyle they wear and the toys they play with. The power of society to influence gender behaviour explains the cases where children have been born with different external sex organs to those that would match their sex determining chromosomes. Despite the influence of their DNA they identify to the gender they have always been told they are. Once the difference has been detected, how then are they ever to feel comfortable in their own skin? The only way to prevent society having such a large influence on gender identity is to allow children to express themselves, wear what they want and play with what they want without fear of not fitting in.

Question 1:

What is the main conclusion from the first paragraph?

A. Society controls gender behaviour.
B. People are different based on their gender.
C. DNA programmes how we act.
D. Boys do not like the same things as girls because of their genes.

Question 2:

Which of the following, if true, points out the flaw in the first paragraph's argument?

A. Not all boys like trucks.
B. Genes control the production of hormones.
C. Differences in gender may be due to an equal combination of society and genes.
D. Some girls like trucks.

Question 3:

According to the statement, how can culture affect identity?

A. Culture can influence what we wear and how we speak.
B. Our parents act the way they do because of culture.
C. Culture affects our genetics.
D. Culture usually relates to where we live.

Question 4:

Which of these is most implied by the statement?

A. Children usually identify with the gender they appear to be.
B. Children are programmed to like the things they do by their DNA.
C. Girls like dollies and pink because their mothers do.
D. It is wrong for boys to have long hair like girls.

Question 5:

What does the statement say is the best way to prevent gender stereotyping?

A. Mothers spending more time with their sons.
B. Parents buying gender-neutral clothes for their children.
C. Allowing children to act how they want.
D. Not telling children if they have different sex organs.

Question 6:

Samantha requires 3 As at A Level to be accepted onto a University course. Samantha is accepted onto the University course, therefore she must have achieved 3 As at A Level.

Which of the following statements most closely follows the reasoning used in this paragraph?

A. A train must pass through Clapham Junction before arriving at Victoria Station. The train passes through Clapham Junction, therefore it will shortly arrive at Victoria Station.
B. If Darlington football club defeat Spennymoor, they will win the league. Darlington defeat Spennymoor, therefore they will win the league.
C. Zeeshan has sold his old car. If he buys a new one, he will go on holiday to London. Zeeshan has gone on holiday to London, therefore he must have bought a new car.
D. Lucy is afraid of flying, but needs to travel on an aeroplane in order to visit Egypt. Lucy has recently visited Egypt, therefore she must have travelled on an aeroplane.
E. If the A1 is open, Andrew will be able to drive to Scotland. However, the A1 is closed due to a traffic collision, so Andrew cannot drive to Scotland.

Questions 7-11 are based on the passage below:

New evidence has emerged that the most important factor in a child's development could be their napping routine. It has come to light that regular napping could well be the deciding factor for determining toddlers' memory and learning abilities. The new countrywide survey of 1000 toddlers, all born in the same year showed around 75% had regular 30-minute naps. Parents cited the benefits of their child having a regular routine (including meal times) such as decreased irritability, and stated the only downfall of occasional problems with sleeping at night. Research indicating that toddlers were 10% more likely to suffer regular night-time sleeping disturbances when they regularly napped supported the parent's view.

Those who regularly took 30-minute naps were more than twice as likely to remember simple words, such as those of new toys, than their non-napping counterparts, who also had higher incidences of memory impairment, behavioural problems and learning difficulties. Toddlers who regularly had 30 minute naps were tested on whether they were able recall the names of new objects the following day, compared to a control group who did not regularly nap. These potential links between napping and memory, behaviour and learning ability provides exciting new evidence in the field of child development.

Question 7:
If in 100 toddlers 5% who did not nap were able to remember a new teddy's name, how many who had napped would be expected to remember?

A. 8   B. 9   C. 10   D. 12

Question 8:

Assuming that the incidence of night-time sleeping disturbances is the same in for all toddlers independent of all characteristics other than napping, what is the percentage of toddlers who suffer regular night-time sleeping disturbances as a result of napping?

A. 7.5%   C. 14%   E. 50%

B. 10%   D. 20%

Question 9:

Using the information from the passage above, which of the following is the most plausible alternative reason for the link between memory and napping?

A. Children who have bad memory abilities are also likely to have trouble sleeping.
B. Children who regularly nap, are born with better memories.
C. Children who do not nap were unable to concentrate on the memory testing exercises for the study.
D. Parents who enforce a routine of napping are more likely to conduct memory exercises with their children.

Question 10:

Which of the following is most strongly indicated?

A. Families have more enjoyable meal times when their toddlers regularly nap.
B. Toddlers have better routines when they nap.
C. Parents enforce napping to improve their toddlers' memory ability.
D. Napping is important for parents' routines.

Question 11:

Which of the following, if true, would strengthen the conclusion that there is a causal link between regular napping and improved memory in toddlers?

A. Improved memory is also associated with regular mealtimes.
B. Parents who enforce regular napping are more inclined to include their children in studies.
C. Toddlers' memory development is so rapid that even a few weeks can make a difference to performance.
D. Among toddler playgroups where napping incidence is higher and more consistent memory performance is significantly improved compared to those that do not.

Question 12:

Tom's father says to him: 'You must work for your A-levels. That is the best way to do well in your A-level exams. If you work especially hard for Geography, you will definitely succeed in your Geography A-level exam'.

Which of the following is the best statement Tom could say to prove a flaw in his father's argument?

A. 'It takes me longer to study for my History exam, so I should prioritise that.'
B. 'I do not have to work hard to do well in my Geography A-level.'
C. 'Just because I work hard, does not mean I will do well in my A-levels.'
D. 'You are putting too much importance on studying for A-levels.'
E. 'You haven't accounted for the fact that Geography is harder than my other subjects.'

Question 13:

Today the NHS is increasingly struggling to be financially viable. In the future, the NHS may have to reduce the services it cannot afford. The NHS is supported by government funds, which come from those who pay tax in the UK. Recently the NHS has been criticised for allowing fertility treatments to be free, as many people believe these are not important and should not be paid for when there is not enough money to pay the doctors and nurses.

Which of the following is the most accurate conclusion of the statement above?

A. Only taxpayers should decide where the NHS spends its money.
B. Doctors and nurses should be better paid.
C. The NHS should stop free fertility treatments.
D. Fertility treatments may have to be cut if finances do not improve.

Question 14:

'We should allow people to drive as fast as they want. By allowing drivers to drive at fast speeds, through natural selection the most dangerous drivers will kill only themselves in car accidents. These people will not have children, hence only safe people will reproduce and eventually the population will only consist of safe drivers.'

Which one of the following, if true, most weakens the above argument?

A. Dangerous drivers harm others more often than themselves by driving too fast.
B. Dangerous drivers may produce children who are safe drivers.
C. The process of natural selection takes a long time.
D. Some drivers break speed limits anyway.

Question 15:

In the winter of 2014, the UK suffered record levels of rainfall, which led to catastrophic damage across the country. Thousands of homes were damaged and even destroyed, leaving many homeless in the chaos that followed. The Government faced harsh criticism that they had failed to adequately prepare the country for the extreme weather. In such cases the Government assess the likelihood of such events happening in the future and balance against the cost of advance measures to reduce the impact should they occur versus the cost of the event with no preparative defences in place.

Until recently, for example, the risk of acts of terror taking was low compared with the vast cost anticipated should they occur. However, the risk of flooding is usually low, so it could be argued that the costs associated with anti-flooding measures would have been pre-emptively unreasonable. Should the Government be expected to prepare for every conceivable threat that could come to pass? Are we to put in place expensive measures against a seismic event as well as a possible extra-terrestrial invasion?

Which of the following best expresses the main conclusion of the statement above?

A. The Government has an obligation to assess risks and costs of possible future events.
B. The Government should spend money to protect against potential extra-terrestrial invasions and seismic events.
C. The Government should have spent money to protect against potential floods.
D. The Government was justified in not spending heavily to protect against flooding.
E. The Government should assist people who lost their homes in the floods.

Question 16:

Sadly the way in which children interact with each other has changed over the years. Where once children used to play sports and games together in the street, they now sit alone in their rooms on the computer playing games on the Internet. Where in the past young children learned human interaction from active games with their friends this is no longer the case. How then, when these children are grown up, will they be able to socially interact with their colleagues?

Which one of the following is the conclusion of the above statement?

A. Children who play computer games now interact less outside of them.
B. The Internet can be a tool for teaching social skills.
C. Computer games are for social development.
D. Children should be made to play outside with their friends to develop their social skills for later in life.
E. Adults will in the future play computer games as a means of interaction.

Question 17:

Between 2006 and 2013 the British government spent £473 million on Tamiflu antiviral drugs in preparation for a flu pandemic, despite there being little evidence to support the effectiveness of the drug. The antivirals were stockpiled for a flu pandemic that never fully materialised. Only 150,000 packs were used during the swine flu episode in 2009, and it is unclear if this improved outcomes. Therefore this money could have been much better spent on drugs that would actually benefit patients.

Which option best summarises the author's view in the passage?
A. Drugs should never be stockpiled, as they may not be used.
B. Spending millions of pounds on drugs should be justified by strong evidence showing positive effects.
C. We should not prepare for flu pandemics in the future.

D. The recipients of Tamiflu in the swine flu pandemic had no difference in symptoms or outcomes to patients who did not receive the antivirals.

Question 18:

High BMI and particularly central weight are risk factors associated with increased morbidity and mortality. Many believe the development of cheap, easily accessible fast-food outlets is partly responsible for the increase in rates of obesity. An unhealthy weight is commonly associated with a generally unhealthy lifestyle, such a lack of exercise. The best way to tackle the growing problem of obesity is for the government to tax unhealthy foods so they are no longer a cheap alternative.

Why is the solution given, to tax unhealthy foods, not a logical conclusion from the passage?

A. Unhealthy eating is not exclusively confined to low-income families.
B. A more general approach to unhealthy lifestyles would be optimal.
C. People do not only choose to eat unhealthy food because it is cheaper.
D. People need to take personal responsibility for their own health.

Question 19:

As people are living longer, care in old age is becoming a larger burden. Many people require carers to come into their home numerous times a day or need full residential care. It is not right that the NHS should be spending vast funds on the care of people who are sufficiently wealthy to fund their own care. Some argue that they want their savings kept to give to their children; however this is not a right, simply a luxury. It is not right that people should be saving and depriving themselves of necessary care, or worse, making the NHS pay the bill, so they have money to pass on to their offspring. People need to realise that there is a financial cost to living longer.

Which of the following statements is the main conclusion of the above passage?

A. We need to take a personal responsibility for our care in old age.
B. Caring for the elderly is a significant burden on the NHS.
C. The reason people are reluctant to pay for their own care is that they want to pass money onto their offspring.
D. The NHS should limit care to the elderly to reduce their costs.
E. People shouldn't save their money for old age.

Question 20:

There is much interest in research surrounding production of human stem cells from non-embryo sources for potential regenerative medicine, and a huge financial and personal gain at stake. In January 2014, a team from Japan published two papers in *Nature* that claimed to have developed totipotent stem cells from adult mouse cells by exposure to an acidic environment. However, there has since been much controversy surrounding these papers. Problems included: inability by other teams to replicate the results of the experiment, an insufficient protocol described in the paper and issues with images in one of the papers. It was dishonest of the researchers to publish the papers with such problems, and a requirement of a paper is a sufficiently detailed protocol, so that another group could replicate the experiment.

Which of the following statements is most implied?

A. Research is fuelled mainly by financial and personal gains.
B. The researchers should take responsibility for publishing the paper with such flaws.
C. Rivalry between different research groups makes premature publishing more likely.
D. The discrepancies were in only one of the papers published in January 2014.

Question 21:

The placebo effect is a well-documented medical phenomenon in which a patient's condition undergoes improvement after being given an ineffectual treatment that they believe to be a genuine treatment. It is frequently used as a control during trials of new drugs/procedures, with the effect of the drug being compared to the effect of a placebo, and if the drug does not have a greater effect than the placebo, then it is classed as ineffective. However, this analysis discounts the fact that the drug treatment still has more of a positive effect than no action, and so we are clearly missing out on the potential to improve certain patient conditions. It follows that where there is a demonstrated placebo effect, but treatments are ineffective, we should still give treatments, as there will therefore be some benefit to the patient.

Which of the following best expresses the main conclusion of this passage?

A. In situations where drugs are no more effective than a placebo, we should still give drugs, as they will be more effective than not taking action.

B. Our current analysis discounts the fact that even if drug treatments have no more effect than a placebo, they may still be more effective than no action.

C. The placebo effect is a well-recognised medical phenomenon.

D. Drugs may have negative side effects that outweigh their benefit.

E. Placebos are better than modern drugs.

Question 22:

The speed limit on motorways and dual carriageways has been 70 mph since 1965, but this is an out-dated policy and needs to change. Since 1965, car brakes have become much more effective, and many safety features have been introduced into cars, such as seatbelts (which are now compulsory to wear), crumple zones and airbags. Therefore, it is clear that cars no longer need to be restricted to 70 mph, and the speed limit can be safely increased to 80 mph without causing more road fatalities.

Which of the following best illustrates an assumption in this passage?

A. The government should increase the speed limit to 80 mph.
B. If the speed limit were increased to 80mph, drivers wouldn't drive at 90.
C. The safety systems introduced reduce the chances of fatal road accidents for cars travelling at higher speeds.
D. The roads have not become busier since the 70 mph speed limit was introduced.
E. The public want the speed limit to increase.

Question 23:

Despite the overwhelming scientific proof of the theory of evolution, and even acceptance of the theory by many high-ranking religious ministers, there are still sections of many major religions that do not accept evolution as true. One of the most prominent of these in western society is the Intelligent Design movement, which promotes the religious-based (and scientifically discredited) notion of Intelligent Design as a scientific theory. Intelligent Design proponents often point to complex issues of biology as proof that god is behind the design of human beings, much as a watchmaker is inherent in the design of a watch.

One part of anatomy that has been identified as supposedly supporting Intelligent Design is fingerprints, with some proponents arguing that they are a mark of individualism created by God, with no apparent function except to identify each human being as unique. This is incorrect, as fingerprints do have a well documented function – namely channelling away of water to improve grip in wet conditions – in which hairless, smooth skinned hands otherwise struggle to grip smooth objects. The individualism of fingerprints is accounted for by the complexity of thousands of small grooves. Development is inherently affected by stochastic or random processes, meaning that the body is unable to uniformly control its development to ensure that fingerprints are the same in each human being. Clearly, the presence of individual fingerprints does nothing to support the so-called-theory of Intelligent Design.

Which of the following best illustrates the main conclusion of this passage?

A. Fingerprints have a well-established function.
B. Evolution is supported by overwhelming scientific proof.
C. Fingerprints do not offer any support to the notion of Intelligent Design.
D. The individual nature of fingerprints is explained by stochastic processes inherent in development that the body cannot uniformly control.
E. Intelligent design is a credible and scientifically rigorous theory.

Question 24:

If the blue party wins the general election, they will implement all of the policies of their manifesto, including an increase in the number of soldiers enlisted in the army. If the army has more soldiers, it will build a new military base in Devon to accommodate them. Therefore, if the blue party wins the election, a new military base will be built in Devon.

Which of the following most closely follows the reasoning used in this argument?

A. If David does not pay his road tax, his car will be confiscated by the local council. If David's car is confiscated, he will not be able to travel to work. Therefore, if David does not pay his road tax, he will lose his job.

B. If a car passes a speed camera whilst travelling at more than 70mph, it will be photographed by the speed camera. If a car is photographed by a speed camera, a speeding ticket will be sent to the owner. Therefore, if John's car is driving along the road at 80mph, he will receive a speeding ticket.

C. If Omar does well in his A Level exam, he will be accepted at Durham University to study classics. If he is accepted at Durham University, he will graduate in Durham Cathedral. Therefore, if Omar does well in his exams, he will graduate in Durham Cathedral.

D. Grace is travelling home from Birmingham. However, the fuel on her car is running low. In order to make it home, she needs to refuel her car. In order for her to refuel her car, she has to leave the motorway and visit a petrol station. Grace arrives home, therefore she must have visited a petrol station.

E. If Country X is further south than Country A, crops will be planted earlier in the year than they are in Country A. If crops are planted earlier, they will be ripe sooner in the year. Crops in Country X are ripe earlier in the year than crops in Country A. Therefore, Country X must be further south than France.

Question 25:

A train is scheduled to depart from Newcastle at 3:30pm. It stops at Durham, Darlington, York, Sheffield, Peterborough and Stevenage before arriving at Kings Cross station in London, where the train completes its journey. The total length of the journey between Newcastle and Kings Cross was 230 miles, and the average speed of the train during the journey (including time spent stood still at calling stations) is 115mph. Therefore, the train will complete its journey at 5:30pm.

Which of the following is an assumption made in this passage?

A. The various stopping points did not increase the time taken to complete the journey.
B. The train left Newcastle on time.
C. The train travelled by the most direct route available.
D. The train was due to end its journey at Kings Cross.
E. There were no signalling problems encountered on the journey.

Question 26:

There have been many arguments over the last couple of decades about government expenditure on healthcare in the various devolved regions of the UK. It is often argued that, since spending on healthcare per person is higher in Scotland than in England, that therefore the people in Scotland will be healthier.

However, this view fails to take account of the different needs of these 2 populations of the UK. For example, one major factor is that Scotland gets significantly colder than England, and cold weakens the immune system, leaving people in Scotland at much higher risk of infectious disease. Thus, Scotland requires higher levels of healthcare spending per person simply to maintain the health of the populace at a similar level to that of England.

Which of the following is a conclusion that can be drawn from this passage?

A. The higher healthcare spending per person in Scotland does not necessarily mean people living in Scotland are healthier.
B. Healthcare spending should be increased across the UK.
C. Wales requires more healthcare spending per person simply to maintain population health at a similar level to England.
D. It is unfair on England that there is more spending on healthcare per person in Scotland.
E. Scotland's healthcare budget is a controversial topic.

Question 27:

Vaccinations have been hugely successful in reducing the incidence of several diseases throughout the 20th century. One of the most spectacular achievements was arguably the global eradication of Smallpox, once a deadly worldwide killer, during the 1970s. Fortunately, there was a highly effective vaccine available for Smallpox, and a major factor in its eradication was an aggressive vaccination campaign. Another disease that is potentially eradicable is Polio.

However, although there is a highly effective vaccine for Polio available, attempts to eradicate it have so far been unsuccessful. It follows that we should plan and execute an aggressive vaccination campaign for Polio, in order to ensure that this disease too is eradicated.

Which of the following is the main conclusion of this passage?

A. Polio is a potentially eradicable disease.
B. An aggressive vaccination campaign was key in the eradication of smallpox.
C. Both Polio and smallpox have been eradicated by vaccination campaigns.
D. We should execute an aggressive vaccination campaign for Polio.
E. The eradication of smallpox remains one of the most spectacular achievements of medical science.

Question 28:

The Y chromosome is one of 2 sex chromosomes found in the human genome, the other being the X chromosome. As the Y chromosome is only found in males, it can only be passed from father to son. Additionally, the Y chromosome does not exchange sections with other chromosomes (as happens with most chromosomes), meaning it is passed on virtually unchanged through the generations. All of this makes the Y chromosome a fantastic tool for genetic analysis, both to identify individual lineages and to investigate historic population movements. One famous achievement of genetic research using the Y chromosome provides further evidence of its utility, namely the identification of Genghis Khan as a descendant of up to 8% of males in 16 populations across Asia.

Which of the following best illustrates the main conclusion of this passage?

A. The Y chromosome is a fantastic tool for genetic analysis.
B. Research using the Y chromosome has been able to identify Genghis Khan as the descendant of up to 8% of men in many Asian populations.
C. The Y chromosome does not exchange sections with other chromosomes.
D. The Y chromosome is a sex chromosome.

Question 29:

In order for a bacterial infection to be cleared, a patient must be treated with antibiotics. Rachel has a minor lung infection, which is thought by her doctor to be a bacterial infection. She is treated with antibiotics, but her condition does not improve. Therefore, it must not be a bacterial infection.

Which of the following best illustrates a flaw in this reasoning?

A. It assumes that a bacterial infection would definitely improve after treatment with antibiotics.
B. It ignores the other potential issues that could be treated by antibiotics.
C. It assumes that antibiotics are necessary to treat bacterial infections.
D. It ignores the actions of the immune system, which may be sufficient to clear the infection regardless of what has caused it.
E. It assumes that antibiotics are the only option to treat a bacterial infection.

Question 30:

The link between smoking and lung cancer has been well established for many decades by overwhelming numbers of studies and conclusive research. The answer is clear and simple, that the single best measure that can be taken to avoid lung cancer is to not smoke, or to stop smoking if one has already started.

However, despite the overwhelming evidence and clear answers, many smokers continue to smoke, and seek to minimise their risk of lung cancer by focusing on other, less important risk factors, such as exercise and healthy eating. This approach is obviously severely flawed, and the fact that some smokers feel this is a good way to reduce their risk of lung cancer shows that they are delusional.

Which of the following best illustrates the main conclusion of this passage?

A. Many smokers ignore the largest risk factor, and focus on improving less important risk factors by eating healthily and exercising.
B. Some smokers are delusional.
C. The biggest risk factor of lung cancer is smoking.
D. Overwhelming studies have proven the link between smoking and lung cancer.
E. The government should ban smoking in order to reduce the incidence of lung cancer.

Question 31:

The government should invest more money into outreach schemes in order to encourage more people to go to university. These schemes allow students to meet other people who went to university, which they may not always be able to do otherwise, even on open days.

Which of the following is the best conclusion of the above argument?

A. Outreach schemes are the best way to encourage people to go to university.
B. People will not go to university without seeing it first.
C. The government wants more people to go to university.
D. Meeting people who went to a university is a more effective method than university open days.
E. It is easier to meet people on outreach schemes than on open days.

Question 32:

The illegal drug cannabis was recently upgraded from a class C drug to class B, which means it will be taken less in the UK, because people will know it is more dangerous. It also means if people are caught, possessing the drug they will face a longer prison sentence than before, which will also discourage its use.

Which **TWO** statements if true, most weaken the above argument?

A. Class C drugs are cheaper than class B drugs.
B. Upgrading drugs in other countries has not reduced their use.
C. People who take illegal drugs do not know what class they are.
D. Cannabis was not the only class C drug before it was upgraded.
E. Even if they are caught possessing class B drugs, people do not think they will go to prison.

Question 33:

Schools with better sports programmes such as well-performing football and netball teams tend to have better academic results, less bullying and have overall happier students. Thus, if we want schools to have the best results, reduce bullying and increase student happiness, teachers should start more sports clubs.

Which one of the following best demonstrates a flaw in the above argument?

A. Teachers may be too busy to start sports clubs.
B. Better academic results may be a precondition of better sports teams.
C. Better sports programmes may prevent students from spending time with their family.
D. Some sports teams may be seen to encourage internal bullying.
E. Sport teams that do not perform well lead to increase bullying.

Question 34:

The legal age for purchasing alcohol in the UK is 18. This should be lowered to 16 because the majority of 16 year olds drink alcohol anyway without any fear of repercussions. Even if the police catch a 16-year-old buying alcohol, they are unable to enforce any consequences. If the drinking limit was lowered the police could spend less time trying to catch underage drinkers and deal with other more important crimes. There is no evidence to suggest that drinking alcohol at 16 is any more dangerous than at 18.

Which one of the following, if true, most weakens the above argument?

A. Most 16 year olds do not drink alcohol.
B. If the legal drinking age were lowered to 16, more 15 year olds would start purchasing alcohol.
C. Most 16 year olds do not have enough money to buy alcohol.
D. Most 16 year olds are able to purchase alcohol currently.

Question 35:

There has been a recent change in the way the government helps small businesses. Whilst previously small businesses were given non-repayable grants to help them grow their profits, they can now only receive government loans that must be repaid with interest when the business turns a certain amount of profit. The government wants to support small businesses but studies have shown they are less likely to prosper under the new scheme as they have been deterred from taking government money for fear of loan repayments.

Which one of the following can be concluded from the passage above?

A. Small businesses do not want government money.
B. The government cannot afford to give out grants to small businesses anymore.
C. All businesses avoid accumulating debt.
D. The action of the government is more likely to do more harm than good to small businesses.
E. Big businesses do not need government money.

Questions 36-41 are based on the passage below:

Despite the numerous safety measures in place within the practice of medicine, these can fail when the weaknesses in the layers of defence aligns to create a clear path leading to often disastrous results. This is known as the 'Swiss cheese model of accident causation'. One such occurrence occurred where the wrong kidney was removed from a patient due to a failure in the line of defences designed to prevent such an incident occurring.

When a kidney is diseased it is removed to prevent further complications, this operation, a 'nephrectomy', is regularly performed by experienced surgeons. Where normally the consultant who knew the patient would have conducted the procedure, in this case he passed the responsibility to his registrar, who was also well experienced but had not met the patient previously. The person who had copied out the patient's notes had poor handwriting had accidentally written the 'R' for 'right' in such a way that it was read as an 'L' and subsequently copied, and not noticed by anyone who further reviewed the notes. The patient had been put asleep before the registrar had arrived and so he proceeded without checking the procedure with the patient, as he normally would have done. The nurses present noticed this error but said nothing, fearing repercussions for questioning a senior professional.

A medical student was present whom, having met the patient previously in clinical, tried to alert the registrar to the mistake he was about to make. The registrar shouted at the student that she should not interrupt surgery; she did not know what she was talking about and asked her to leave. Consequently the surgery proceeded with the end result being that the patient's healthy left kidney was removed, leaving them with only their diseased right kidney, which would eventually lead to the patient's unfortunate death. Frightening as these cases appear what is perhaps scarier is the thought of how those reported may be just the 'tip of the iceberg'.

When questioned about his action to allow his registrar to perform the surgery alone, the consultant had said that it was normal to allow capable registrars to do this. 'While the public perception is that medical knowledge steadily increases over time, this is not the case with many doctors reaching their peak in the middle of their careers.' He had found that his initial increasing interest in surgery had enhanced his abilities, but with time and practice the similar surgeries had become less exciting and so his lack of interest had correlated with worsening outcomes, thus justifying his decision to devolve responsibility in this case.

Question 36:

Which of the following, if true, most weakens the argument above?

A. If incidences are severe enough to occur, they will be reported.

B. Doctors undergo extensive training to reduce risks.

C. Thousands of operations happen every year with no problems.

D. Some errors are unavoidable.

E. The patient could have possibly passed away even if the operation had been a complete success.

Question 37:

Which one of the following is the overall conclusion of the statement?

A. The error that occurred was a result of the failure of safety precautions in place.

B. Surgeries should only be performed by surgeons who know their patients well.

C. The human element to medicine means errors will always occur.

D. The safety procedures surrounding surgical procedures need to be reviewed.

E. Some doctors are overconfident.

Question 38:

Which of the following is attributed as the original cause of the error?

A. The medical student not having asserted herself.

B. The poor handwriting in the chart.

C. The hierarchical system of medicine.

D. The registrar not having met the patient.

E. The patient being asleep.

F. The lack of the surgical skill possessed by the registrar.

G. The registrar's poor attitude.

Question 39:

What does the 'tip of the iceberg' refer to in the passage?

A. Problems we face every day.
B. The probable large numbers of medical errors that go unreported.
C. The difficulties of surgery.
D. Reported medical errors.
E. Problems within the NHS.

The following graphs are needed for Questions 40-41:

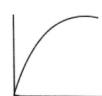
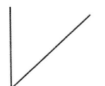

Question 40:

Which graph best describes the consultants' performance versus emotional arousal over his career?

A. A   B. B   C. C   D. D   E. E   F. F

Question 41:

Which graphs best describe the medical knowledge acquired over time?

Option	Public's Perception	Consultant's Perception
A	B	B
B	B	D
C	B	F
D	D	B
E	D	D
F	D	F
G	F	B
H	F	D
I	F	F

Question 42:

Sadly, in recent times, the lack of exercise associated with sedentary lifestyles has increased in the developed world. The lack of opportunity for exercise is endemic and these countries have also seen a rise of diseases such as diabetes even in young people. In these developed countries, bodily changes such as increased blood pressure, that are usually associated with old age, are rapidly increasing. These are however still uncommon in undeveloped countries, where most people are physically active throughout the entirety of their lives.

Which one of the following can be concluded from the passage above?

A. Exercise has a greater effect on old people than young people.
B. Maintenance of good health is associated with lifelong exercise.
C. Changes in lifestyle will be necessary to cause increased life expectancies in developed countries.
D. Exercise is only beneficial when continued into old age.
E. Obesity and diabetes are the result of lack of exercise.

Questions 43 -45 are based on the passage below:

'Midwives should now encourage women to, as often as possible, give birth at home. Not only is there evidence to suggest that normal births at home are as safe those as in hospital, but it removes the medicalisation of childbirth that emerged over the years. With the increase in availability of health resources we now, too often, use services such as a full medical team for a process that women have been completing single-handedly for thousands of years.

Midwives are extensively trained to assist women during labour at home and capable enough to assess when there is a problem that requires a hospital environment. Expensive hospital births must and should move away from being standard practice, especially in an era where the NHS has far more demands on its services that it can currently afford.'

Question 43:

Which of the following is the most appropriate conclusion from the statement?

A. People are over dependent on healthcare.
B. Some women prefer to have their babies in hospital.
C. Having a baby in hospital can actually be more risky than at home.
D. Childbirth has been over medicalised.
E. Encouraging women to have their babies at home may relieve some of the financial pressures on the NHS.
F. We should have more midwives than doctors.

Question 44:

Which one of the following if true most weakens the argument in the passage?

A. Some women are scared of home births.
B. Home births are associated with poorer outcomes.
C. Midwives do not like performing home visits.
D. Some home births result in hospital births anyway.

Question 45:

Which one of the following describes what the statement cites as the cause for the 'medicalisation of childbirth'?

A. Women fear giving birth without a full medical team present.

B. Midwives are incapable of aiding childbirth without help.

C. Giving birth at home is not as safe as it used to be.

D. Excessive availability of health services.

Question 46:

We need to stop focussing so much attention on the dangers of fires. In 2011 there were only 242 deaths due to exposure to smoke, fire and flames, while there were 997 deaths from hernias. We need to think more proportionally as these statistics show that campaigns such as 'fire kills' are not necessary as comparison with the risk from the death from hernias clearly shows that fires are not as dangerous as they are perceived to be.

Which of the following statements identify a weakness in the above argument?

1. More people may die in fires if there were no campaigns about their danger and how to prevent them.

2. The smoke of a fire is more dangerous than it flames.

3. There may be more people with hernias than those in fires.

A. I only
B. 2 only
C. 3 only
D. I and 2 only

E. I and 3 only
F. 2 and 3 only
G. I, 2 and 3

Question 47:

A survey of a school was taken to find out whether there was any correlation between the sports students played and the subjects they liked. The findings were as follows: some football players liked Maths and some of them liked History. All students liked English. None of the basketball players liked History, but all of them, as well as some rugby players liked Chemistry. All rugby players like Geography.

Based on the findings, which one of the below must be true?

A. Some of the footballers liked Maths and History.
B. Some of the rugby players liked three subjects.
C. Some rugby players liked History.
D. Some of the footballers liked English but did not like Maths and History.
E. Some basketball players like more than 3 subjects.

Question 48:

The control of illegal drug use is becoming increasingly difficult. New 'legal highs' are being manufactured which are slightly changed molecularly from illegal compounds so they are not technically illegal. These new 'legal drugs' are being brought onto the street at a rate of at least one per week, and so the authorities cannot keep up.

Some health professionals therefore believe that the legality of drugs is becoming less relevant as to the potentially dangerous side effects. The fact that these new compounds are legal may however mean that the public are not aware of their equally high risks.

Which of the following are implied by the argument?

1. Some health professionals believe there is no value in making drugs illegal.
2. The major problem in controlling illegal drug use is the rapid manufacture of new drugs that are not classified as illegal.
3. The general public are not worried about the risks of legal or illegal highs.
4. There is no longer a good correlation between risk of drug taking and the legal status of the drug.

A. 1 only
B. 2 only
C. 1 and 4
D. 2 and 4
E. 2 and 3
F. 1, 2, 3 and 4

Question 49:

WilderTravel Inc. is a company which organises wilderness travel holidays, with activities such as trekking, mountain climbing, safari tours and wilderness survival courses. These activities carry inherent risks, so the directors of the company are drawing up a set of health regulations, with the aim of minimising the risks by ensuring that nobody participates in activities if they have medical complications meaning that doing so may endanger them.

They consider the following guidelines:

'Persons with pacemakers, asthma or severe allergies are at significant risk of heart attack in low oxygen environments'. People undertaking mountain climbing activities with WilderTravel frequently encounter environments with low oxygen levels. The directors therefore decide that in order to ensure the safety of customers on WilderTravel holidays, one step that must be taken is to bar those with pacemakers, asthma or allergies from partaking in mountain climbing.

Which of the following best illustrates a flaw in this reasoning?

A. Participants should be allowed to assess the safety risks themselves, and should not be barred from activities if they decide the risk is acceptable.
B. They have assumed that all allergies carry an increased risk of heart attack, when the guidelines only say this applies to those with severe allergies.
C. The directors have failed to consider the health risks of people with these conditions taking part in other activities.
D. People with these conditions could partake in mountain climbing with other holiday organisers, and thus be exposed to danger of heart attack.

Question 50:

St John's Hospital in Northumbria is looking to recruit a new consultant cardiologist, and interviews a series of candidates. The interview panel determines that 3 candidates are clearly more qualified for the role than the others, and they invite these 3 candidates for a second interview. During this second interview, and upon further examination of their previous employment records, it becomes apparent that Candidate 3 is the most proficient at surgery of the 3, whilst Candidate 1 is the best at patient interaction and explaining the risks of procedures. Candidate 2, meanwhile, ranks between the other 2 in both these aspects.

The hospital director tells the interviewing team that the hospital already has a well-renowned team dedicated to patient interaction, but the surgical success record at the hospital is in need of improvement. The director issues instructions that therefore, it is more important that the new candidate is proficient at surgery, and patient interaction is less of a concern.

Which of the following is a conclusion that can be drawn from the Directors' comments?

A. The interviewing team should hire Candidate 2, in order to achieve a balance of good patient relations with good surgical records.
B. The interviewing team should hire Candidate 1, in order to ensure good patient interactions, as these are a vital part of a doctor's work.
C. The interviewing team should ignore the hospital director and assess the candidates further to see who would be the best fit.
D. The interviewing team should hire Candidate 3, in order to ensure that the new candidate has excellent surgical skills, to boost the hospital's success in this area.

Question 51:

Every winter in Britain, there are thousands of urgent callouts for ambulances in snowy conditions. The harsh conditions mean that ambulances cannot drive quickly, and are delayed in reaching patients. These delays cause many injuries and medical complications, which could be avoided with quicker access to treatment. Despite this, very few ambulances are equipped with winter tyres or special tyre coverings to help the ambulances deal with snow. Clearly, if more ambulances were fitted with winter tyres, then we could avoid many medical complications that occur each winter.

Which of the following is an assumption made in this passage?

A. Fitting winter tyres would allow ambulances to reach patients more quickly.
B. Ambulance trusts have sufficient funding to equip their vehicles with winter tyres.
C. Many medical complications could be avoided with quicker access to medical care.
D. There are no other alternatives to winter tyres that would allow ambulances to reach patients more quickly in snowy conditions.

Question 52:

Vaccinations have been one of the most outstanding and influential developments in medical history. Despite the huge successes, however, there is a strong anti-vaccination movement active in some countries, particularly the USA, who claim vaccines are harmful and ineffective.

There have been several high-profile events in recent years where anti-vaccine campaigners have been refused permission to enter countries for campaigns, or have had venues refuse to host them due to the nature of their campaigns. Many anti-vaccination campaigners have claimed this is an affront to free speech, and that they should be allowed to enter countries and obtain venues without hindrance. However, although free speech is desirable, an exception must be made here because the anti-vaccination campaign spreads misinformation to parents, causing vaccination to rates to drop.

When this happens, preventable infectious diseases often begin to increase, causing avoidable deaths of innocent members of the community, particularly so in children. Thus, in order to protect innocent people, we must continue to block the anti-vaccine campaigners from spreading misinformation freely by pressuring venues not to host anti-vaccination campaigners.

Which of the following best illustrates the principle that this argument follows?

A. Free speech is always desirable, and must not be compromised under any circumstances.

B. The right of innocent people to protection from infectious diseases is more important than the right of free speech.

C. The right of free speech does not apply when the party speaking is lying or spreading misinformation.

D. Public health programmes that achieve significant success in reducing the incidence of disease should be promoted.

Question 53:

In order for a tumour to grow larger than a few centimetres, it must first establish its own blood supply by promoting angiogenesis. Roger has a tumour in his abdomen, which is investigated at the Royal General Hospital. During the tests, they detect newly formed blood vessels in the tumour, showing that it has established its own blood supply. Thus, we should expect the tumour to grow significantly, and become larger than a few centimetres. Action must be taken to deal with this.

Which of the following **best** illustrates a flaw in this reasoning?

A. It assumes that the tumour in Roger's abdomen has established its own blood supply.
B. It assumes that a blood supply is necessary for a tumour to grow larger than a few centimetres.
C. It assumes that nothing can be done to stop the tumour once a blood supply has been established.
D. It assumes that a blood supply is sufficient for the tumour to grow larger than a few centimetres.

Question 54:

In this year's Great North Run, there are several dozen people running to raise money for the Great North Air Ambulance (GNAA), as part of a large national fundraising campaign. If the runners raise £500,000 between them, then the GNAA will be able to add a new helicopter to its fleet. However, the runners only raise a total of £420,000. Thus, the GNAA will not be able to get a new helicopter.

Which of the following **best** illustrates a flaw in this passage?

A. It has assumed that the GNAA will not be able to acquire a new helicopter without the runners raising £500,000.
B. It has assumed that that GNAA wishes to add a new helicopter to its fleet.

C. It has assumed that the GNAA does not have better things to spend the money on.

D. It has assumed that some running in the Great North Run are raising money for the GNAA.

Question 55:

Many courses, spanning Universities, colleges, apprenticeship institutions and adult skills courses should be subsidised by the government. This is because they improve the skills of those attending them. It has been well demonstrated that the more skilled people are, the more productive they are economically. Thus, government subsidies of many courses would increase overall economic productivity, and lead to increased growth.

Which of the following would most weaken this argument?

A. The UK already has a high level of growth, and does not need to accelerate.

B. Research has demonstrated that higher numbers of people attending adult skills courses results in increased economic growth.

C. Research has demonstrated that the cost of many courses (to those taking them) has little effect on the number of people undertaking the courses.

D. Employers often seek to employ those with greater skill-sets, and appoint them to higher positions.

Question 56:

Pluto was once considered the 9th planet in the solar system. However, further study of the planet led to it being reclassified as a dwarf planet in 2006, due to the discovery of many objects in the solar system with similar characteristics to Pluto, which were also placed into this new category of 'Dwarf Planet'. Some astronomers believe that Pluto should remain classified as a planet, along with the many entities similar to Pluto that have been discovered. It is clear that if we were to reclassify Pluto as a planet, and maintain consistency with classification of astronomical entities, then the number of planets would significantly increase.

Which of the following best illustrates the main conclusion of this passage?

A. If Pluto is classified as a planet, then many other entities should also be planets, as they share similar characteristics.
B. Some astronomers believe Pluto should be classified as a planet.
C. Pluto should not be classified as a Planet, as this would also require many other entities to be classified as planets to ensure consistency.
D. If Pluto is to be classified as a planet, then the number of objects classified as planets should increase significantly.

Question 57:

2 trains depart from Birmingham at 5:30 pm. One of the trains is heading to London, whilst the other is heading to Glasgow. The distance from Birmingham to Glasgow is three times larger than the distance from Birmingham to London, and the train to London arrives at 6:30 pm. Thus, the train to Glasgow will arrive at 8:30pm.

Which of the following is an assumption made in this passage?

A. Both trains depart at the same time.
B. Both trains depart from Birmingham.
C. Both trains travel at the same speed.
D. The train heading to Glasgow has to travel three times as far as the train heading to London.

Question 58:

Carcinogenesis, oncogenesis and tumorigenesis are various names given to the generation of cancer, with the term literally meaning 'creation of cancer'. In order for carcinogenesis to happen, there are several steps that must occur. Firstly, a cell (or group of cells) must achieve immortality, and escape senescence (the inherent limitation of a cell's lifespan). Then they must escape regulation by the body, and begin to proliferate in an autonomous way. They must also become immune to apoptosis and other cell death mechanisms. Finally, they must avoid detection by the immune system, or survive its responses. If a single one of these steps fails to occur, then carcinogenesis will not be able to occur.

Which of the following is a conclusion that can be reliably drawn from this passage?

A. Several steps are essential for carcinogenesis.
B. If all the steps mentioned occur, then carcinogenesis will definitely occur.
C. The immune system is unable to tackle cells that have escaped regulation by the body.
D. There are various mechanisms by which carcinogenesis can occur.
E. The terminology for the creation of cancer is confusing.

Question 59:

P53 is one of the most crucial genes in the body, responsible for detecting DNA damage and halting cell replication until repair can occur. If repair cannot take place, P53 will signal for the cell to kill itself. These actions are crucial to prevent carcinogenesis, and a loss of functional P53 is identified in over 50% of all cancers. The huge importance of P53 towards protecting the cell from damaging mutations has led to it deservedly being known as 'the guardian of the genome'. The implications of this name are clear – any cell that has a mutation in P53 is at serious risk of developing a potentially dangerous mutation.

Which of the following **CANNOT** be reliably concluded from this passage?

A. P53 is responsible for detecting DNA damage.
B. Most cancers have lost functional P53.
C. P53 deserves its name 'guardian of the genome'.
D. A cell that has a mutation in P53 will develop damaging mutations.
E. None of the above.

Question 60:

Sam is buying a new car, and deciding whether to buy a petrol or a diesel model. He knows he will drive 9,000 miles each year. He calculates that if he drives a petrol car, he will spend £500 per 1,000 miles on fuel, but if he buys a diesel model he will only spend £300 per 1,000 miles on fuel. He calculates, therefore, that if he purchases a Diesel car, then this year he will make a saving of £1800, compared to if he bought the petrol car.

Which of the following is **NOT** an assumption that Sam has made?

A. The price of diesel will not fluctuate relative to that of petrol.
B. The cars will have the same initial purchase cost.
C. The cars will have the same costs for maintenance and garage expenses.
D. The cars will use the same amount of fuel.
E. All of the above are assumptions.

Question 61:

In the UK, cannabis is classified as a Class B drug, with a maximum penalty of up to 5 years imprisonment for possession, or up to 14 years for possession with intent to supply. The justification for drug laws in the UK is that classified drugs are harmful, addictive, and destructive to people's lives. However, available medical evidence indicates that cannabis is relatively safe, non-addictive and harmless. In particular, it is certainly shown to be less dangerous than alcohol, which is freely sold and advertised in the UK. The fact that alcohol can be freely sold and advertised, but cannabis, a less harmful drug, is banned highlights the gross inconsistencies in UK drugs policy.

Which of the following best illustrates the main conclusion of this passage?

A. Cannabis is a less dangerous drug than alcohol.
B. Alcohol should be banned, so we can ensure consistency in the UK drug policy.
C. Cannabis should not be banned, and should be sold freely, in order to ensure consistency in the UK drug policy.
D. The UK government's policy on drugs is grossly inconsistent.
E. Alcohol should not be advertised in the UK.

Question 62:

Every year in Britain, there are thousands of accidents at people's homes such as burns, broken limbs and severe cuts, which cause a large number of deaths and injuries. Despite this, very few households maintain a sufficient first aid kit equipped with bandages, burn treatments, splints and saline to clean wounds. If more households stocked sufficient first aid supplies, many of these accidents could be avoided.

Which of the following best illustrates a flaw in this argument?

A. It ignores the huge cost associated with maintaining good first aid supplies, which many households cannot afford.
B. It implies that presence of first aid equipment will lead to fewer accidents.
C. It ignores the many accidents that could not be treated even if first aid supplies were readily available.
D. It neglects to consider the need for trained first aid persons in order for first aid supplies to help in reducing the severity of injuries caused by accidents.

Question 63:

Researchers at SmithJones Inc., an international drug firm, are investigating a well-known historic compound, which is thought to reduce levels of DNA replication by inhibiting DNA polymerases. It is proposed that this may be able to be used to combat cancer by reducing the proliferation of cancer cells, allowing the immune system to combat them before they spread too far and become too damaging. Old experiments have demonstrated the effectiveness of the compound via monitoring DNA levels with a dye that stains DNA red, thus monitoring the levels of DNA present in cell clusters. They report that the compound is observed to reduce the rate at which DNA replicates.

However, it is known that if researchers use the wrong solutions when carrying out these experiments, then the amount of red staining will decrease, suggesting DNA replication has been inhibited, even if it is not inhibited. As several researchers previously used this wrong solution, we can conclude that these experiments are flawed, and do not reflect what is actually happening.

Which of the following best illustrates a flaw in this argument?

A. From the fact that the compound inhibits DNA replication, it cannot be concluded that it has potential as an anticancer drug.
B. From the fact that the wrong solutions were used, it cannot be concluded that the experiments may produce misleading results.
C. From the fact that the experiments are old, it cannot be concluded that the wrong solutions were used.
D. From the fact that the compound is old, it cannot be concluded that it is safe.

Question 64:

Rotherham football club are currently top of the league, with 90 points. Their closest competitors are South Shields football club, with 84 points. Next week, the teams will play each other, and after this, they each have 2 games left before the end of the season. Each win is worth 3 points, a draw is worth 1 point, and a loss is worth 0 points. Thus, if Rotherham beat South Shields, they will win the league (as they will then be 9 points clear, and South Shields would only be able to earn 6 more points).

In the match of Rotherham vs. South Shields, Rotherham are winning until the 85th minute, when Alberto Simeone scores an equaliser for South Shields, and South Shields then go on to win the match. Thus, Rotherham will not win the league.

Which of the following best illustrates a flaw in this passage's reasoning?

A. It has assumed that Alberto Simeone scored the winning goal for South Shields.
B. It has assumed that beating South Shields was necessary for Rotherham to win the league, when in fact it was only sufficient.
C. Rotherham may have scored an equaliser later in the game, and not lost the match.
D. It has failed to consider what other teams might win the league.

Question 65:

Oakville Supermarkets is looking to build a new superstore, and a meeting of its directors has been convened to decide where the best place to build the supermarket would be. The Chairperson of the Board suggests that the best place would be Warrington, a town that does not currently have a large supermarket, and would thus give them an excellent share of the shopping market.

However, the CEO notes that the population of Warrington has been steadily declining for several years, whilst Middlesbrough has recently been experiencing high population growth. The CEO therefore argues that they should build the new supermarket in Middlesbrough, as they would then be within range of more people, and so of more potential customers.

Which of the following best illustrates a flaw in the CEO's reasoning?

A. Middlesbrough may already have other supermarkets, so the new superstore may get a lower share of the town's shoppers.
B. Despite the recent population changes, Warrington may still have a larger population than Middlesbrough.
C. Middlesbrough's population is projected to continue growing, whilst Warrington's is projected to keep falling.
D. Many people in Warrington travel to Liverpool or Manchester, 2 nearby major cities, in order to do their shopping.

Question 66:

Global warming is a key challenge facing the world today, and the changes in weather patterns caused by this phenomenon have led to the destruction of many natural habitats, causing many species to become extinct. Recent data has shown that extinctions have been occurring at a faster rate over the last 40 years than at any other point in the earth's history, exceeding the great Permian mass extinction, which wiped out 96% of life on earth. If this rate continues, over 50% of species on earth will be extinct by 2100. It is clear that in the face of this huge challenge, conservation programmes will require significantly increased levels of funding in order to prevent most of the species on earth from becoming extinct.

Which of the following are assumptions in this argument?

1. The rate of extinctions seen in the last 40 years will continue to occur without a step-up in conservation efforts.
2. Conservation programmes cannot prevent further extinctions without increased funding.
3. Global warming has caused many extinction events, directly or indirectly.

A. 1 only
B. 2 only
C. 3 only
D. 1 and 2

E. 1 and 3
F. 2 and 3
G. 1, 2 and 3

Question 67:

After an election in Britain, the new government is debating what policy to adopt on the railway system, and whether it should be entirely privatised, or whether public subsidies should be used to supplement costs and ensure that sufficient services are run. Studies in Austria, which has high public funding for railways, have shown that the rail service is used by many people, and is highly thought of by the population. However, this is clearly down to the fact that Austria has many mountainous and high-altitude areas, which experience significant amounts of snow and ice. This makes many roads impassable, and travelling by road difficult. Thus, rail is often the only way to travel, explaining the high passenger numbers and approval ratings. Thus, the high public subsidies clearly have no effect.

Which of the following, if true, would weaken this argument?

1. France also has high public subsidy of railways, but does not have large areas where travel by road is difficult. The French railway also has high passenger numbers and approval ratings.
2. Italy also has high public subsidy of railways, but the local population dislike using the rail service, and it has poor passenger numbers.
3. There are many reasons affecting the passenger numbers and approval ratings of a given country's rail serviced.

A. 1 only   C. 3 only   E. 1 and 3
B. 2 only   D. 1 and 2   F. 2 and 3

Questions 68 & 69 are based on the passage below:

Tobacco companies sell cigarettes despite being fully aware that cigarettes cause significant harm to the wellbeing of those that smoke them. Diseases caused or aggravated by smoking cost billions of pounds for the NHS to treat each year. This is extremely irresponsible behaviour from the tobacco companies. Tobacco companies should be taxed, and the money raised put towards funding the NHS.

Question 68:

Which of these following arguments best illustrates the principle used in this argument?

A. Many homeless people in the UK cannot afford medical treatment. This is morally outrageous, as many are homeless through no fault of their own. Therefore, we should tax the rich in the UK, and use the money to fund medical treatment for the homeless.

B. Alcohol induced diseases such as liver failure cost significant amounts to treat, and put a large strain on the NHS. Therefore, people who drink heavily and then suffer from alcohol induced diseases should be made to pay for their own medical treatment.

C. Many people are poor due to spending large amounts of money on gambling or other wasteful obsessions. People such as this, who are poor through their own fault, should not receive free medical treatment. Free medical treatment should only go to those who cannot afford it through no fault of their own.

D. People who use private healthcare providers should not be forced to pay taxes that go towards funding the NHS. People should only be forced to contribute money to the NHS if they use the services it provides.

E. Fireworks are responsible for starting large numbers of fires each year, killing many people and putting a significant strain on the fire service. Despite this, companies continue to sell fireworks. Therefore, companies selling fireworks should be taxed to provide extra funding for the fire service.

Question 69:

Which of the following conclusions **CANNOT** be drawn from the above?

A. There is a connection between lung cancer and smoking.
B. There is a connection between liver disease and smoking.
C. There is a connection between oral cancer and smoking.
D. All smokers drink excessively.
E. All of the above.

Question 70:

Investigations in the origins of species suggest that humans and the great apes have the same ancestors. This is suggested by the high degree of genetic similarity between humans and chimpanzees (estimated at 99%). At the same time there is an 84% homology between the human genome and that of pigs. This raises the interesting question of whether it would be possible to use pig or chimpanzee organs for the treatment of human disease.

Which conclusion can be reasonably drawn from the above article?

A. Pigs and chimpanzees have a common ancestor.
B. Pigs and humans have a common ancestor.
C. It can be assumed that chimpanzees will develop into humans if given enough time.
D. There seems to be great genetic homology across a variety of species.
E. Organs from pigs or chimpanzees present a good alternative for human organ donation.

Question 71:

Poor blood supply to a part of the body can cause damage of the affected tissue - i.e. lead to an infarction. There are a variety of known risk factors for vascular disease. Diabetes is a major risk factor. Other risk factors are more dependent on the individual as they represent individual choices such as smoking, poor dietary habits as well as little to no exercise. In some cases infarction of the limbs and in particular the feet can become very bad and extensive with patches of tissue dying. This is known as necrosis and is marked by affected area of the body turning black. Necrotic tissue is usually removed in surgery.

Which of the following statements **CANNOT** be concluded from the information in the above passage?

A. Smoking causes vascular disease.
B. Diabetes causes vascular disease.
C. Vascular disease always leads to infarctions.
D. Necrotic tissue must be removed surgically.
E. Necrotic tissue only occurs following severe infarction.
F. All of the above

Question 72:

People who can afford to pay for private education should not have access to the state school system. This would allow more funding for students from lower income backgrounds. More funding will provide better resources for students from lower income backgrounds, and will help to bridge the gap in educational attainment between students from higher income and lower income backgrounds.

Which of the following statements, if true, would most strengthen the above argument?

A. Educational attainment is a significant factor in determining future prospects.
B. Providing better resources for students has been demonstrated to lead to an increase in educational attainment.
C. Most people who can afford to do so choose to purchase private education for their children.
D. A significant gap exists in educational attainment between students from high income and low-income backgrounds.
E. Most schools currently receive a similar amount of funding relative to the number of students in the school.

Question 73:

Increasing numbers of people are choosing to watch films on DVD in recent years. In the past few years, cinemas have lost customers, causing them to close down. Many cinemas have recently closed, removing an important focal point for many local communities and causing damage to those communities. Therefore, we should ban DVDs in order to help local communities.

Which of the following best states an assumption made in this argument?

A. The cinemas that have recently closed have done so because of reduced profits due to people choosing to watch DVDs instead.
B. Cinemas being forced to close causes damage to local communities.
C. DVDs are improving local communities by allowing people to meet up and watch films together.
D. Sales of DVDs have increased due to economic growth.
E. Local communities have called for DVDs to be banned.

Question 74:

Aeroplanes are the fastest form of transport available. An aeroplane can travel a given distance in less time than a train or a car. John needs to travel from Glasgow to Birmingham. If he wants to arrive as soon as possible, he should travel by aeroplane.

Which of the following best illustrates a flaw in this argument?

A. One day, there could be faster cars built that could travel as fast as aeroplanes.
B. Travelling by air is often more expensive.
C. It ignores the time taken to travel to an airport and check in to a flight, which may mean he will arrive later if travelling by aeroplane.
D. John may not own a car, and thus may not have any option.
E. John may not be legally allowed to make the journey.

Question 75:

During autumn, spiders frequently enter people's homes to escape the cold weather. Many people dislike spiders and seek ways to prevent them from entering properties, leading to spider populations falling as they struggle to cope with the cold weather. Studies have demonstrated that when spider populations fall, the population of flies rises. Higher numbers of flies are associated with an increase in food poisoning cases. Therefore, people must not seek to prevent spiders from entering their homes.

Which of the following best illustrates the main conclusion of this argument?

A. People should not dislike spiders being present in their homes.
B. People should seek methods to prevent flies from entering their homes.
C. People should actively encourage spiders to occupy their homes to increase biodiversity.
D. People should accept the presence of spiders in their homes to reduce the incidence of food poisoning.
E. Spiders should be cultivated and used as a biological pest control to combat flies.

Question 76:

Each year, thousands of people acquire infections during prolonged stays at hospital. Concurrently, bacteria are becoming resistant to antibiotics at an ever-increasing rate. In spite of this, progressively less pharmaceutical companies are investing in research into new antibiotics, and the number of antibiotics coming onto the market is decreasing. As a result, the number of antibiotics that can be used to treat infections is falling. If pharmaceutical companies were pressured into investing in new antibiotic research, many lives could be saved.

Which of the following best illustrates a flaw in this argument?

A. It assumes the infections acquired during stays at hospital are resulting in deaths.
B. It ignores the fact that many people never have to stay in hospital.
C. It does not take into account the fact that antibiotics do not produce much profit for pharmaceutical companies.
D. It ignores the fact that some hospital-acquired infections are caused by organisms that cannot be treated by antibiotics, such as viruses.
E. It assumes that bacterial resistance to antibiotics has not been happening for some time.

Question 77:

Katherine has shaved her armpits most of her adult life, but has now decided to stop. She explains her reasons for this to John, saying she does not like the pressures society puts on women to be shaven in this area. John listens to her reasons, but ultimately responds 'just because you explain why I should find your hairiness attractive, it does not mean I will. I find you unattractive, as I do not like girls with hair on their arm pits.'

What assumption has John made?

A. That just because he finds Katherine unattractive, he would find other girls with unshaven arm pits unattractive.
B. That Katherine is trying to make John find her armpit hair attractive.
C. That Katherine will never conceal her armpit hair.
D.   Katherine must be wrong, because she is a woman.
E. That Katherine thinks women should stop shaving.

Question 78:

Medicine has improved significantly over the last century. Better medicine causes a reduction in the death rate from all causes. However, as people get older, they suffer from infectious disease more readily.

Many third world countries have a high rate of deaths from infectious disease. Sunita argues that this high death rate is caused by better medicine, which has given an ageing population, thus giving a high rate of deaths from infectious disease as elderly people suffer from infectious disease more readily. Sunita believes that better medicine is thus indirectly responsible for this high death rate from infectious disease.

However, this cannot be the case. In third world countries, most people do not live to old age, often dying from infectious disease at a young age. Therefore, an ageing population cannot be the reason behind the high rate of death from infectious disease. As better medicine causes a reduction in the death rate from all causes, it is clear that better medicine will lead to a reduction in the death rate from infectious disease in third world countries.

Which of the following best states the main conclusion of this argument?

A. We can expect that improvements in medicine seen over the last century will improve.
B. Better medicine is not responsible for the increased prevalence of infectious disease in third world countries.
C. Better medicine has caused the overall death rate of third world countries to increase.
D. Better medicine will cause a decrease in the rate of death from infectious disease in third world countries.
E. As people get older, they suffer from infectious disease more readily.

Question 79:

Bristol and Cardiff are 2 cities with similar demographics, and located in a roughly similar area of the country. Bristol has higher demand for housing than Cardiff. Therefore, a house in Bristol will cost more than a similar house in Cardiff.

Which of the following best illustrates an assumption in the statement above?

A. House prices will be higher if demand for housing is higher.
B. People can commute from Cardiff to Bristol.
C. Supply of housing in Cardiff will not be lower than in Bristol.
D. Bristol is a better place to live.
E. Cardiff has sufficient housing to provide for the needs of its communities.

Question 80:

Jellicoe Motors is a small motor company in Sheffield, employing 3 people. The company is hiring a new mechanic and interviews several candidates. New research into production lines has indicated that having employees with a good ability to work as part of a team boosts a company's productivity and profits. Therefore, Jellicoe motors should hire a candidate with good team-working skills.

Which of the following best illustrates the main conclusion of this argument?

A. Jellicoe Motors should not hire a new mechanic.
B. Jellicoe motors should hire a candidate with good team-working skills in order to boost their productivity and profits.
C. Jellicoe motors should hire several new candidates in order to form a good team, and boost their productivity.
D. If Jellicoe motors does not hire a candidate with good team-working skills, they may struggle to be profitable.
E. Jellicoe motors should not listen to the new research.

Question 81:

Research into new antibiotics does not normally hold much profit for pharmaceutical firms. As a consequence many firms are not investing in antibiotic research, and very few new antibiotics are being produced. However, with bacteria becoming increasingly resistant to current antibiotics, new ones are desperately needed to avoid running the risk of thousands of deaths from bacterial infections. Therefore, the UK government must provide financial incentives for pharmaceutical companies to invest in research into new antibiotics.

Which of the following best expresses the main conclusion of this argument?

A. If bacteria continue to become resistant to antibiotics, there could be thousands of deaths from bacterial infections.
B. Pharmaceutical firms are not investing in new antibiotic research due to a lack of potential profit.
C. If the UK government invests in research into new antibiotics, thousands of lives will be saved.
D. The pharmaceutical firms should invest in areas of research that are profitable, and ignore antibiotic research.

E. The UK government must provide financial incentives for pharmaceutical firms to invest into antibiotic research if it wishes to avoid risking thousands of deaths from bacterial infections.

Question 82:

People in developing countries use far less water per person than those in developed countries. It is estimated that at present, people in the developing world use an average of 30 litres of water per person per day, whilst those in developed countries use on average 70 litres of water per person per day. It is estimated that for the current world population, an average water usage of 60 litres per person per day would be sustainable, but any higher than this would be unsustainable.

The UN has set development targets such that in 20 years, people living in developing countries will be using the same amount of water per person per day as those living in developed countries. Assuming the world population stays constant for the next 20 years, if these targets are met the world's population will be using water at an unsustainable rate.

Which of the following, if true, would most weaken the argument above?

A. The prices of water bills are dropping in developed countries like the UK.
B. The level of water usage in developed countries is falling, and may be below 60 litres per person per day in 20 years.
C. The population of all developing countries is less than the population of all developed countries.
D. Climate change is likely to decrease the amount of water available for human use over the next 20 years.
E. The UN's development targets are unlikely to be met.

Question 83:

In this Senior Management post we need someone who can keep a cool head in a crisis and react quickly to events. The applicant says he suffers from a phobia about flying, and panics especially when an aircraft is landing and that therefore he would prefer not to travel abroad on business if it could be avoided. He is obviously a very nervous type of person who would clearly go to pieces and panic in an emergency and fail to provide the leadership qualities necessary for the job. Therefore this person is not a suitable candidate for the post.

Which of the following highlights the biggest flaw in the argument above?

A. It falsely assumes phobias are not treatable or capable of being eliminated.
B. It falsely assumes that the person appointed to the job will need to travel abroad.
C. It falsely assumes that a specific phobia indicates a general tendency to panic.
D. It falsely assumes that people who stay cool in a crisis will be good leaders.
E. It fails to take into account other qualities the person might have for the post.

Question 84:

There are significant numbers of people attending university every year, as many as 45% of 18 year olds. As a result, there are many more graduates entering the workforce with better skills and better earning potential. Going to university makes economic sense and we should encourage as many people to go there as possible.

Which of the following highlights the biggest flaw in the argument above?

A. There are no more university places left.
B. Students can succeed without going to university.

C. Not all degrees equip students with the skills needed to earn higher salaries.
D. Some universities are better than others.

Question 85:

Young people spend too much time watching television, which is bad for them. Watching excessive amounts of TV is linked to obesity, social exclusion and can cause eye damage. If young people were to spend just one evening a week playing sport or going for a walk the benefits would be manifold. They would lose weight, feel better about themselves and it would be a sociable activity. Exercise is also linked to strong performance at school and so young people would be more likely to perform well in their exams.

Which of the following highlights the biggest flaw in the argument above?

A. Young people can watch sport on television.
B. There are many factors that affect exam performance.
C. Television does not necessarily have any damaging effect.
D. Television and sport are not linked.

Question 86:

Campaigners pushing for legalisation of cannabis have many arguments for their cause. Most claim there is little evidence of any adverse effects to health caused by cannabis usage, that many otherwise law-abiding people are users of cannabis and that in any case, prohibition of drugs does not reduce their usage. Legalising cannabis would also reduce crime associated with drug trafficking and would provide an additional revenue stream for the government.

Which of the following best represents the conclusion of the passage?

A. Regular cannabis users are unlikely to have health problems.
B. Legalising cannabis would be good for cannabis users.
C. There are multiple reasons to legalise cannabis.

D. Prohibition is an effective measure to reduce drugs usage.

E. Drug associated crime would reduce if cannabis was legal.

Question 87:

Mohan has been offered a new job in Birmingham, starting in several months with a fixed salary. In order to ensure he can afford to live in Birmingham on his new salary, Mohan compares the prices of some houses in Birmingham. He finds that a 2 bedroomed house will cost £200,000. A 3 bedroomed house will cost £250,000. A 4 bedroomed house with a garden will cost £300,000.

Mohan's bank tells him that if he is earning the salary of the job he has been offered, they will grant him a mortgage for a house costing up to £275,000. After a month of deliberation, Mohan accepts the job and decides to move to Wolverhampton. He begins searching for a house to buy. He reasons that he will not be able to purchase a 4-bedroomed house.

Which of the following is **NOT** an assumption that Mohan has made?

A. A house in Wolverhampton will cost the same as a similar house in Birmingham.

B. A different bank will not offer him a mortgage for a more expensive house on the same salary.

C. The salary for the job could increase, allowing him to purchase a more expensive house.

D. A 4-bedroomed house without a garden will not cost less than a 4-bedroomed house with a garden.

E. House prices in Birmingham will not have fall in the time between now and Mohan purchasing a house.

Question 88:

We should teach the Holocaust in schools. It is important that young people see what it was like for Jewish people under Nazi rule. If we expose the harsh realities to impressionable people then this will help improve tolerance of other races. It will also prevent other such terrible events happening again.

Which is the best conclusion?

A. We should teach about the Holocaust in schools.
B. The Holocaust was a tragedy.
C. The Nazis were evil.
D. We should not let terrible events happen again.
E. Educating people is the best solution to the world's problems.

Question 89:

The popular series 'Game of Thrones' should not be allowed on television because it shows scenes of a disturbing nature, in particular scenes of rape. Children may find themselves watching the programme on TV, and then going on to commit the terrible crime of rape, mimicking what they have watched.

Which of the following best illustrates a flaw in this argument?

A. Children may also watch the show on DVD.
B. Adults may watch the show on television.
C. Watching an action does not necessarily lead to recreating the action yourself.
D. There are lots of non-violent scenes in the show.

Question 90:

The TV series 'House of Cards' teaches us all a valuable lesson: the world is not a place that rewards kind behaviour. The protagonist of the series, Frank Underwood, uses intrigue and guile to achieve his goals, and through clever political tactics he is able to climb in rank. If he were to be kinder to people, he would not be able to be so successful. Success is predicated on his refusal to conform to conventional morality. The TV series should be shown to small children in schools, as it could teach them how to achieve their dreams.

Which of the following is an assumption made in the argument?

A.   Children pay attention to school lessons.
B.   The TV series is sufficiently entertaining.
C.   One cannot both obey a moral code and succeed.
D.   Frank Underwood is a likable character.

Question 91:

Freddy makes lewd comments on a female passer-by's body to his friend, Neil, loud enough for the woman in question to hear. Neil is uncomfortable with this, and states that it is inappropriate for Freddy to do so, and that Freddy is being sexist. Freddy refutes this, and Neil retorts that Freddy would not make these comments about a man's body. Freddy replies by saying 'it is not sexist, I am a feminist, I believe in equality for men and women.'

Which of the following describes a flaw made in Freddy's logic?

A.   A self-proclaimed feminist could still say a sexist thing.
B.   The female passer-by in question felt uncomfortable.
C.   Neil, too, considers himself a feminist.
D.   It would still not be okay to make lewd comments at male passers-by.
E.   Lewd comments are always inappropriate.

Question 92:

The release of CO_2 from consumption of fossil fuels is the main reason behind global warming, which is causing significant damage to many natural environments throughout the world. One significant source of CO_2 emissions is cars, which release CO_2 as they use up petrol. In order to tackle this problem, many car companies have begun to design cars with engines that do not use as much petrol. However, engines which use less petrol are not as powerful, and less powerful cars are not attractive to the public. If a car company produces cars which are not attractive to the public, they will not be profitable.

Which of the following best illustrates the main conclusion of this argument?

A. Car companies making cars that use less petrol aren't profitable.
B. The public prefer more powerful cars.
C. Car companies should prioritise profits over helping the environment.
D. Car companies should seek to produce engines that use less petrol but are still just as powerful.
E. The public are not interested in helping the environment.

Question 93:

A group of scientists investigates the role of different nutrients after exercise. They set up two groups of averagely fit individuals consisting of the same number of both males and females aged 20 – 25 and weighing between 70 and 85 kilos. Each group will conduct the same 1hr exercise routine of resistance training, consisting of various weighted movements. After the workout they will receive a shake with vanilla flavour that has identical consistency and colour in all cases. Group A will receive a shake containing 50 g of protein and 50g of carbohydrates. Group B will receive a shake containing 100 g of protein and 50 g of carbohydrates. All participants have their lean body mass measured before starting the experiment.

Which of the following statements is correct?

A. The experiment compares the response of men and women to endurance training.
B. The experiment is flawed as it does not take into consideration that men and women respond differently to exercise.
C. The experiment does not consider age.
D. The experiment mainly looks at the role of protein after exercise.
E. None of the above.

Question 94:

It may amount to millions of pounds each year of taxpayers' money; however, it is strongly advisable for the HPV vaccination in schools to remain. The vaccine, given to teenage girls, has the potential to significantly reduce cervical cancer deaths and furthermore, the vaccines will decrease the requirement for biopsies and invasive procedures related to the follow-up tests. Extensive clinical trials and continued monitoring suggest that both Gardasil and Cervarix are safe and tolerated well by recipients. Moreover, studies demonstrate that a large majority of teenage girls and their parents are in support of the vaccine.

Which of the following is the conclusion of the above argument?

A. HPV vaccines are safe and well tolerated
B. It is strongly advisable for the HPV vaccination in schools to remain
C. The HPV vaccine amounts to millions of pounds each year of taxpayers' money
D. The vaccine has the potential to significantly reduce cervical cancer deaths
E. Vaccinations are vital to disease prevention across the population

Question 95:

Until the twentieth century, the whole purpose of art was to create beautiful, flawless works. Artists attained a level of skill and craft that took decades to perfect and could not be mirrored by those who had not taken great pains to master it. The serenity and beauty produced from movements such as impressionism has however culminated in repulsive and horrific displays of rotting carcasses designed to provoke an emotional response rather than admiration. These works cannot be described as beautiful by either the public or art critics. While these works may be engaging on an intellectual or academic level, they no longer constitute art.

Which of the following is an assumption of the above argument?

A. Beauty is a defining property of art.
B. All modern art is ugly.
C. Twenty first century artists do not study for decades.
D. The impressionist movement created beautiful works of art.
E. Some modern art provokes an emotional response.

Question 96:

The consumption of large quantities of red meat is suggested to have negative health ramifications. Carnitine is a compound present in red meat and a link has been discovered between carnitine and the development of atherosclerosis, involving the hardening, and narrowing of arteries. Intestinal bacteria convert carnitine to trimethylamine-N-oxide, which has properties that are damaging to the heart. Moreover, red meat consumption has been associated with a reduced life expectancy. It may be that charring meat generates toxins that elevate the chance of developing stomach cancer. If people want to be healthy, a vegetarian diet is preferable to a diet including meat. Vegetarians often have lower cholesterol and blood pressure and a reduced risk of heart disease.

Which of the following is an assumption of the above argument?

A. Diet is essential to health and we should all want to be healthy.
B. Vegetarians do the same amount of exercise as meat eaters.
C. Meat has no health benefits.
D. People who eat red meat die earlier.
E. Red meat is the best source of iron.

Question 97:
Many people believe that foreign travel broadens the mind and that there is some inherent benefit in spending some time in a culture different from your own. Many students are taking 'gap' years where they spend time in another country. Whilst this may offer some benefits in terms of confidence and independence, it is wrong to assume that foreign travel alone can provide this. Global travel can have negative impacts on local cultures and the environment. Home country based 'gap' projects are often seen as unglamorous, but the benefit of working with different groups of people and different cultures within our own society can be equally rewarding.

Which one of the following is the main conclusion of the above passage?

A. Foreign gap year projects must have an element of community work for them to be worthwhile.
B. Foreign travel is not the only way to gain confidence and independence.
C. Projects within our own society can be as rewarding as foreign travel.
D. There is inherent benefit in spending some time abroad.
E. It is important that gap year students consider the impact of their travel on the communities they work in.

Question 98:

"Bottled water is becomingly increasingly popular, but it is hard to see why. Bottled water costs many hundreds of times more than a virtually identical product from the tap, and bears a significant environmental cost of transportation. Those who argue in favour of bottled water may point out that the flavour is slightly better – but would you pay 300 times the price for a car with just a few added features?"

Which of the following, if true, would most weaken the above argument?

A. Bottled water has many health benefits in addition to tasting nicer
B. Bottled water does not taste any different to tap water
C. The cost of transportation is only a fraction of the costs associated with bottling and selling water
D. Some people do buy very expensive cars
E. Buying bottled water supports a big industry, providing many jobs to people

Question 99:

Up until the 20th century, all watches were made by hand, by watchmakers. Watchmaking is considered one of the most difficult and delicate of manufacturing skills, requiring immense patience, meticulous attention to detail and an extremely steady hand. However, due to the advent of more accurate technology, most watches are now produced by machines, and only a minority are made by hand, for specialist collectors. Thus, some watchmakers now work for the watch industry, and only perform *repairs* on watches that are initially produced by machines.

Which of the following *cannot* be reliably concluded from this passage?

A. Most watches are now produced by machines, not by hand.
B. Watchmaking is considered one of the most difficult of manufacturing skills

C. Most watchmakers now work for the watch industry, performing repairs on watches rather than producing new ones.
D. The advent of more accurate technology caused the situation today, where most watches are made by machines.
E. Some watches are now made by hand for specialist collectors.

Question 100:

Many vegetarians claim that they do not eat meat, poultry or fish because it is unethical to kill a sentient being. Most agree that this argument is logical. However, some Pescatarians have also used this argument, that they do not eat meat because they do not believe in killing sentient beings, but they are happy to eat fish. This argument is clearly illogical. There is powerful evidence that fish fulfil just as much of the criteria for being sentient as do most commonly eaten animals, such as chicken or pigs, but that all these animals lack certain criteria for being "sentient" that humans possess. Thus, pescatarians should either accept the killing of beings less sentient than humans, and thus be happy to eat meat and poultry, or they should not accept the killing of any partially sentient beings, and thus not be happy to eat fish.

Which of the following best illustrates the main **conclusion** of this passage?

A. The argument that it is unethical to eat meat due to not wishing to kill sentient beings but eating fish is acceptable is illogical.
B. Pescatarians cannot use logic.
C. Fish are just as sentient as chicken and pigs, and all these beings are less sentient than humans.
D. It is not unethical to eat meat, poultry or fish.
E. It is unethical to eat all forms of meat, including fish and poultry.

WORKED ANSWERS

Q	A	Q	A	Q	A	Q	A
1	A	31	A	61	D	91	A
2	C	32	C&E	62	B	92	A
3	A	33	B	63	C	93	D
4	A	34	B	64	B	94	B
5	C	35	D	65	B	95	A
6	D	36	A	66	D	96	A
7	D	37	A	67	E	97	C
8	A	38	B	68	E	98	A
9	A	39	D	69	D	99	C
10	B	40	A	70	D	100	A
11	D	41	B	71	F		
12	C	42	B	72	B		
13	D	43	E	73	A		
14	A	44	B	74	C		
15	D	45	D	75	D		
16	A	46	E	76	A		
17	B	47	B	77	B		
18	B	48	D	78	D		
19	A	49	B	79	A		
20	B	50	D	80	B		
21	A	51	A	81	E		
22	C	52	B	82	B		
23	C	53	D	83	C		
24	C	54	A	84	C		
25	B	55	C	85	D		
26	A	56	D	86	C		
27	D	57	C	87	C		
28	A	58	A	88	A		
29	A	59	D	89	C		

Question 1: A
Whilst **B**, **C** and **D** may be true, they are not completely stated, **A** is clearly stated and so is the correct answer.

Question 2: C
The main argument of the first paragraph is to propose the point that it is more society that controls gender behaviour not genetics. **A** and **D** do not indicate either as they only allude to the end result of gender behaviour and so are incorrect. Hormonal effects are not mentioned in the first paragraph and so **B** is incorrect. **C** would undermine the argument that society *predominately* controls gender, and so is correct.

Question 3: A
B, C and **D** are not stated and so are incorrect. **A** is directly stated and so is correct.

Question 4: A
B and **D** are contraindicated by the statement and so are incorrect. **C** could be true but implies children always like the same thing as their same-gendered parent irrelevant of how they are treated as a child, which is contrary to the statement and so is not correct. **A** is correct as is the overall message.

Question 5: C
D may help prevent problems with sexual identity but does not prevent stereotyping and so is incorrect. **A** is not stated, and **B** is implied but not stated and so are incorrect. **C** is the end message of how to prevent gender stereotyping and so is correct.

Question 6: D
The argument follows the reasoning of "A **must** happen for B to happen. B happens, therefore A **must** have happened". Only D) follows this reasoning. Answers A), C) and E) are incorrect, as the conclusions they draw do not necessarily follow from the events described in the sentence. Meanwhile, B) reasons as "If A happens, B **will** happen".

This is not the same as saying that A **must** happen for B to happen. In B), Darlington may have won the league anyway, so the reasoning is not the same as in the question.

Question 7: D

The text states that 'Those who regularly took 30-minute naps were more than twice as likely to remember simple words such as those of new toys.' Which means those who napped were twice as likely to remember teddy's name than the 5% who did not, 5% x 2 = 10%, which would be twice as likely, ruling out **A** and **B**. But being 'more than twice' the only possible answer is **D.**

Question 8: A

The answer is to work out 10% (the percentage of napping toddlers more likely to suffer night disturbances) of 75% (the percentage of toddlers who regularly nap). Hence 10 % of 75% is 7.5%

Question 9: A

B, C and **D** may be true but there is nothing in the text to support them. **A** is suggested, as the passage states 'non-napping counterparts, who also had higher incidences of memory impairment, behavioural problems and learning difficulties'. If the impaired memory were the cause, as opposed to the result, of irregular sleeping then it would offer an alternative reason why those who nap less remember less.

Question 10: B

A and **C** are possible implications but not stated and so are incorrect. It is said that parents cite napping having 'the benefits of their child having a regular routine' so hence **B** is more correct than **D** as it refers to the benefit to the toddlers' rather than the parents.

Question 11: D

B, if true would counteract the conclusion, as it would imply that, the study is skewed. The same is true of **C**, which if true would imply unreliable results as the toddler sample are all the same age within a year, but not within a few weeks. **A,** if true, would not provide any additional support to the conclusion and so is incorrect. **D** if true would provide the most support for the conclusion as it proposes using groups with a higher incidence of napping in comparison to those with a lower incidence.

Question 12: C

Although it can be argued that **A, B, D** and **E** are true they are not the best answer to demonstrate a flaw in Tom's father's argument. **C** is the best because it accounts for other factors determining success for the Geography A-level exam such as aptitude for the subject.

Question 13: D

A is never stated and is incorrect. **B** and **C** are referred to being 'many people's' beliefs, and are cited as others' opinions not an argument supported by evidence in the passage, and so are not valid conclusions. It is implied that the NHS may have to reduce its services in the future, some of which could be fertility treatments hence **D** is the most correct answer.

Question 14: A

C does not severely affect the strength of the argument, as it is only relevant to the length of the time taken for the effects of the argument to come into place. **D** is incorrect, as people breaking speed limits already would not negate the argument that speed limits should be removed, but could even be seen as supporting it. These people may count as the 'dangerous drivers' who would be ultimately weeded out of the population.

B may affect part of the argument's logic (as it undermines the idea that dangerous drivers are born to dangerous drivers), but the final conclusion that dangerous drivers will end up killing only themselves still stands, and so the ultimate population of only safe drivers may be obtained. The fact that one dead dangerous driver could have produced a safe one does not necessarily challenge the main point of this argument.

A if true would most weaken the argument as it states that fast driver is more likely to harm others and not the driver itself, which would negate the whole argument.

Question 15: D
Whilst is it stated that the Government assesses risk it is not described as an obligation, hence **A** is incorrect. The overall conclusion of the statement is that on balance the Government was justified in not spending money on flooding preparation, as it was unlikely to occur, so **C, B** and **E** are incorrect and **D** is correct.

Question 16: A
C is incorrect and **D** is a possible course of action rather than a conclusion. **B** and **E** are possible inferences but not the conclusion of the statement. The overall conclusion of the statement is that the way that children interact has changed to the solitary act of playing computer games.

Question 17: B
The passage does state that in this case the £473 million could have been put to better use, however, there is no mention that no drug should ever be stockpiled for a similar possible pandemic. The passage discusses the lack of evidence behind Tamiflu and therefore is stating that in a situation where there is a lack of evidence, there may not be justification for stockpiling millions of pounds worth of the drug. Stockpiling in the case of drugs with high effectiveness is not discussed so we should not assume this is a generic argument against preparation for any pandemic and stockpiling of any drug.

Question 18: B

The passage discusses the fact that unhealthy eating is associated with other aspects of an unhealthy lifestyle so the argument that tackling only the unhealthy eating aspect does not logically follow. The other statements are all possible reasons why the solution may not be optimal but are not directly referred to in the passage.

Question 19: A

This is a tricky question in which **A**, **B**, **C** and **D** are all true. However, the question asks for the conclusion of the passage, which is best represented by **A**. **B** is a premise that gives justification for why the elderly should take care of themselves and **C** provides a justification for why they may not.

D is implied in the text but statement **A** is explicitly stated. **E** is incorrect as the passage implies that people should spend the money that they have in old age, not stop saving altogether.

Question 20: B

The passage states stem cell research is an area where there are possible high financial and personal gains, however there is no mention of these being the main driving factors in either this area of research or others. Although rivalry between groups may be a reason driving publishing, this is not mentioned in the passage. The image discrepancies were in only one paper but the passage implies the protocol and replication problems were in both papers.

Question 21: A

D actually weakens the argument, and is therefore not a conclusion. **C** is simply a fact stated to introduce the argument, and is not a conclusion. **B** is a reason given in the passage to support the main conclusion. If we accept **B** as being true, it helps support the statement in **A**. **E** is not discussed in the passage. **A** is the main conclusion of this passage

Question 22: C

The passage describes improved safety features and better brakes in cars, and concludes that this means the road limit could be increased to 80mph without causing more road fatalities. However, if **C** is not true, this conclusion no longer follows on from this reasoning. At no point is it stated that **C** is true, so **C** is therefore the assumption in the passage. The statements in **B** and **D** are not *required* to be true for the argument's conclusion to lead on from its reasoning. **A** is a statement which is strengthened by this passage, and is not an assumption from the passage. **E** is not relevant to the conclusion or mentioned in the passage.

Question 23: C

Answers **A** and **D** are both reasons given to explain fingerprints under the theory of evolution, and contribute towards the notion given in **C**, that they do not offer support to intelligent design. Thus, **A** and **D** are reasons given in the passage, and **C** is the main conclusion. **B** is simply a fact stated to introduce the passage, whilst **E** actually contradicts something mentioned in the argument (namely that Intelligent Design is religious-based, and scientifically discredited). Neither of these options are conclusions.

Question 24: C

The question follows the reasoning of "**If** A happens, B **will** happen. **If** B happens, **C will** happen. Therefore, **If** A happens, C **will** happen". Only C) follows this reasoning correctly.

A) and B) are both incorrect because they assume things will happen which have not been stated in the reasoning. In A), it is not stated that David will lose his job if he cannot travel to work, therefore this is incorrect. In B), John's car may not necessarily pass a speed camera, so B) is incorrect. E) also contains incorrect reasoning. It is not stated that either of the things mentioned are *necessary* for crops to be ripe earlier, so we cannot know from what is stated that Country X is further south than Country A.

D) is correct, but follows different reasoning. D) reasons as "A **must** happen for B to happen. B **must** happen for C to happen. Therefore if C happens, A **must** have happened". This is not the same as saying If A happens, B **will** happen. Grace could visit a petrol station yet still not arrive home.

Question 25: B

The passage states that the average speed *including* time spent stood still at stations was 115mph. Thus, **A** is incorrect, as the stopping points have already been included in the calculations of journey time. Similarly, the passage states that the train completes its journey at Kings cross, so **D** is incorrect. **C** is not correct because we have been given the total length of the journey. Whether it took the most direct route is irrelevant. **E** is completely irrelevant and does not affect the answer. **B** is an assumption, because we have only been given the *scheduled* time of departure. If the train was delayed in leaving, it would not have left at 3:30, and so would have arrived *after* 5:30.

Question 26: A

The argument discusses healthcare spending in England and Scotland, and whether this means the population in Scotland will be healthier. It says nothing about whether this system is fair, and does not mention the expenditure in Wales. Thus, **C** and **D** are incorrect. Similarly, the argument makes no reference to whether healthcare spending should be increased, so **B** is incorrect. **E** is true but not the main message of the passage. The passage does suggest that the higher healthcare expenditure per person in Scotland does not necessarily mean that the Scottish population will be healthier, so **A** is a conclusion from this passage.

Question 27: D

C is an incorrect statement, as the passage says that Polio *hasn't* been eradicated yet. **A** and **B** are reasons given to support the conclusion, which is that given in **D**. **E**, meanwhile, is an opinion given in the passage, and is not relevant to the passage's conclusion.

Question 28: A

This passage provides various positive points of the Y chromosome, before describing how all of this means it is a fantastic tool for genetic analysis. Thus, the conclusion is clearly that given in **A**. The statement in **B** is a further point given to provide evidence of its utility, as stated in the passage. Thus **B** is not a conclusion in itself, but further evidence to support the main conclusion, given in **A**. **C** is also a reason given to support the conclusion in **A**, whilst **D** is simply a fact stated to introduce the passage. As for **E,** there is no mention of Genghis Khan's children (only his descendants).

Question 29: A

Answers **C** and **E** are not valid assumptions because the argument has *stated* that a patient *must* be treated with antibiotics for a bacterial infection to clear. B is not a flaw, because this does not affect whether the antibiotics would clear the infection if it were bacterial. D is an irrelevant statement, and also disagrees with a stated phrase in the passage (that antibiotics are required to clear a bacterial infection). A is a valid flaw, because the passage does not say that antibiotics are *sufficient* or *guaranteed* to clear a bacterial infection, simply that they are *necessary*. Thus, it is possible that the infection *is* bacterial but the antibiotics failed to clear it.

Question 30: B

A, **C** and **D**, if accepted as true, all contribute towards supporting the statement given in **B**, which is a valid conclusion given in this passage. Thus, **A**, **C** and **D** are all reasons given to support the main conclusion, which is the statement given in **B**. **E** is not a valid conclusion, as the passage makes no reference to action that should be taken relating to smoking, it simply discusses its position as the main risk factor for lung cancer.

Question 31: A

D is only given as a method, with no mention of its effectiveness. We do not know if **C** is true because it is not stated. **B** is not discussed in the passage. Whilst statement **E** is true, it is supporting evidence for the conclusion, not the conclusion itself.

Question 32: C & E

Whilst **A** and **B** may be true, cost is not mentioned as a deterring factor and we are only concerned with use in the UK, so they are irrelevant. Whether cannabis was the only class C drug is not important to the argument so **D** is not correct. **C** and **E** are the correct answers because the statement concerns the use of cannabis in the UK, directly stating use will decrease from people knowing it has been upgraded to a more dangerous category and from fearing longer prison sentences from higher-class drugs.

Question 33: B

Whilst **A** and **C** may be true, they are not part of the argument. **D** is a possible, but cannot be logically proposed from the information above. **E** would be a flaw if the argument were 'all levels of sports teams reduce bullying' but the passage explicitly states 'well-performing' teams. Hence **B** is correct as it undermines the whole argument, reversing the cause and effect.

Question 34: B

Options **A, C** and **D** do not directly weaken the argument as if any 16-year-olds were buying/drinking alcohol (whether the minority or majority) – police would still be spending time catching them. The suggested benefit to reduce police time spent catching underage drinkers would be negated if **B** were true, hence it is the correct answer.

Question 35: D

A is an interpretation of the last sentence and doesn't accurately summarise the argument in the passage. **B** is untrue as there is no mention of if the government can afford to give grants or not. **C** and **E** are incorrect as the passage only talks about small businesses. **D** is correct as it best summarises the change in government policy regarding small businesses.

Question 36: A

The statement discusses a case that was reported, but aims to argue that there may be important errors occurring everyday in medicine that go unreported. Option **A** if true, would significantly weaken this argument as would negate it being a possibility. **B, C, D** and **E** may be true, but they do not negate the argument – if doctors are trained, accidents like the above may still occur. Operations that are successful do not affect those that are not, nor do unavoidable errors have any relation to avoidable ones. That the patient may have died without these errors similarly does not mean that errors, when they do occur, should not be considered errors.

Question 37: A

The main point of the statement is to highlight that although there are numerous safety precautions in place to protect patients, when the weaknesses in these precautions align big errors can occur. So **A** is correct. While **E, C, B** and **D** may well be true, they are not the overall conclusion of the statement.

Question 38: B

Though not the first to be cited, the original error is cited as being the incorrect copying of the sidedness of the kidney to be removed, hence **B** is the correct option. The other options represent errors that in the 'Swiss cheese model' would have not been allowed to occur if the original had not taken place.

Question 39: D

In this instance the 'tip of the iceberg' refers to the number of medical errors reported, implying there may be a significantly larger proportion that go unreported, hence the correct option is **D**, and not **B**.

Question 40: A

The description given about the consultant's performance versus emotional arousal, is described as initially increasing then eventually decreasing over time, which is best represented by graph **A**.

Question 41: B

The consultant says that the 'public perception is that medical knowledge increases steadily over time' which is best represented by graph **B**. The consultant says that, in terms of medical knowledge, 'many doctors [reach] their peak in the middle of their careers', which is best described by the graph **D**.

Question 42: B

Obesity is not mentioned in the passage, so **E** is incorrect. There is no mention exercise specifically as it relates to old age, so **A** and **D** are also wrong. The diseases associated with lack of exercise are not specifically stated to cause early death, only that they are associated with older people, so **C** is also incorrect. The passage does, however, argue that lack of exercise is associated with illness, and so exercise would be linked to a lack of illness, or good health.

Question 43: E

The preference of women to have their babies at hospital versus home is not commented upon so **B** is incorrect. **F** is never inferred, only that midwives are capable of assisting in normal births and assessing when women need to be transferred to be to hospital, so it is wrong. **A** and **D** are possible inferences at certain points but not conclusions of the statement. **C** is never implied, only that normal home births are no more risky than those in hospital. The overall conclusion of the statement is that the home births should be encouraged where possible as they are not more risky in the cases of normal births, and hospital births are an unsustainable cost in cash-strapped NHS.

Question 44: B

While **A**, **C** and **D** would, if true, make the practicalities of increasing home births more difficult they would not weaken the argument as **B** would. Where the statement's whole argument rests on home births being as safe as hospital **B**, if true, would negate this.

Question 45: D

The statement says 'With the increase in availability of health resources we now, too often, use services such as a full medical team for a process that women have been completing single-handedly for thousands of years.' Thus implying **D**, 'excessive availability of health resources' is the cause of 'medicalisation of childbirth'.

Question 46: E

1 and **3** identify weaknesses in the argument. If campaigns are what help keep deaths by fire low, they can be seen as 'necessary', and their necessity may be proven by the promisingly low fire-related mortalities. If there are more people with hernias than in fires, more people can possibly die from hernias, but this does not mean the fires are less dangerous to the (fewer) individuals involved in them. **2** is irrelevant, as the argument is about how dangerous fires are in their entirety, not in relation to their constituent parts. Therefore **E**, '1 and 3 only', is correct.

Question 47: B

Since 'some footballers' that like Maths are not necessarily the same 'some' who like History we can exclude **A** and **D**. Equally, while **C** may or may not be true, we are not given any information about rugby players' preference for History, so it is incorrect. We know that all basketball players like English and Chemistry, and that none of them like History, but as we do not know about a third subject they may like **E** is incorrect.

We know all of the rugby players like English and Geography and some of them Chemistry, hence there must be a section of rugby players that like all three subjects so **B** is correct.

Question 48: D

The passage discusses the problems surrounding controlling drugs, and focuses on the rapid manufacture of new 'legal highs': it is therefore implied that this is the current major problem. The passage also suggests that as the authorities cannot keep up with drugs manufacture, the legality of drugs doesn't reflect their risks.

1 is incorrect as the passage says health professionals feel legality is less relevant now, but not that it is not still important. **3** is incorrect as the last sentence says a potential problem of legal highs is that the risks are not as clear, which contradicts the statement that the public are not concerned about any risks.

Question 49: B

The passage is discussing how banning those with the mentioned medical conditions from mountain climbing are *essential* to ensuring safety. It does not claim that this is *sufficient* to ensure safety, simply that it is *necessary*. Thus **C** is irrelevant, as risks from other activities do not affect the risk from mountain climbing. **D** is also irrelevant, because the argument discusses how it is essential to ensure safety of people on WilderTravel holidays, so those using other companies are irrelevant.

A is an irrelevant statement because the passage is discussing what should be done *to ensure safety*, not whether this is the morally correct course of action. Thus, a discussion of whether people should choose to accept the risks is not relevant. However, **B** *is* a flaw, because the guidelines only mention those with *severe* allergies, so thinking those with less severe allergies are in danger is a false assumption that has been made by the directors.

Question 50: D

The hospital director's comments make it abundantly clear that the most important aspect of the new candidate is good surgery skills, because the hospital's surgery success record requires improvement. If we accept his reasoning as being true, then it is clear that the candidate who is most proficient at surgery should be hired, and patient interaction should not be the deciding factor. Thus, Candidate 3 should be hired, as suggested by **D**.

Question 51: A

Answers **B** and **D** are irrelevant to the argument's conclusion, since the argument only talks about how medical complications could be avoided *if* winter tyres were fitted. Whether this is possible (as in **B**) or whether there are other options (as in **D**) are irrelevant to this conclusion. C is not an assumption because the passage states that delays cause many complications, which could be avoided with quicker treatment. However, the argument does not state that winter tyres would allow ambulances to reach patients more quickly, so **A** is an assumption.

Question 52: B

The passage discusses how anti-vaccine campaigns cause deaths by spreading misinformation and reducing vaccination rates. It claims that therefore *in order to protect* people, we should block the campaigners from spreading such misinformation freely. Thus it is made clear that this action should be taken *because the campaigners cause deaths*, not simply because they are spreading misinformation. Thus, **B** is the principle embodied in the passage, and **C** is incorrect. **A** actually demonstrates an opposite principle, whilst **D** is a somewhat irrelevant statement, as the passage makes no reference to whether we should promote successful public health programmes.

Question 53: D

The passage states that the tumour has established its own blood supply (it says this was shown during the testing), and that a blood supply is *necessary* for the tumour to grow beyond a few centimetres. Thus **A** and **B** are not assumptions. **C** is not an assumption, as it actually disagrees with something the passage has implied. The passage has actually said that action *must* be taken, implying that something *can* be done to stop the tumour. However, at no point has it been said that a blood supply is *sufficient* for a tumour to grow larger than a few centimetres. If this is not true, then the argument's conclusion that we should expect the tumour to grow larger than a few centimetres, and that action must be taken, no longer readily follows on from its reasoning. It is possible the tumour will still fail to grow larger than a few centimetres. Thus, **D** is an assumption in the passage, and a flaw in its reasoning.

Question 54: A

D is incorrect, as the passage has stated the runners are people running to raise money for the GNAA. **B** and **C**, meanwhile, are incorrect as the passage is only talking about whether the GNAA *will be able to* get a new helicopter. Thus, references to whether it wishes to, or whether this is the best use of money, are irrelevant. **A**, however, is an assumption on the part of the passage's writer. The passage says that the GNAA will be able to get a helicopter if £500,000 is raised, but this does *not* mean that it won't be able to if the £500,000 is not raised by the runners. It could well be that they secure funding from elsewhere, or that prices drop. The money being *sufficient* to get a new helicopter does not mean it is *necessary* to get one.

Question 55: C

B and **D** somewhat strengthen this argument, suggesting that more people going on courses leads to better growth, and that people who have gone on these courses are more attractive to employers. **A** does not really affect the strength of the argument, as the current rate of growth does not affect whether government subsidies would lead to increased growth.

C, however, weakens the argument significantly by suggesting that people would not be more likely to attend the courses if the government were to subsidise them, as the cost has little effect on the numbers of people attending.

Question 56: D

B is simply a fact stated in the passage. It does not draw upon any other reasons given in the passage, so it is not a conclusion. **C** is not a conclusion because it does not follow on from the passage's reasoning. The passage discusses what should be done *if* Pluto is to be classified as a planet, it does not make any mention of whether this *should* happen. **A** and **D** are both valid conclusions from the passage. However, on closer examination we can see that if we accept **A** as being true, it gives us good reason to believe the statement in **D**. Thus, **D** is the *main* conclusion in the passage, whilst **A** is an *intermediate* conclusion, which supports this main conclusion.

Question 57: C

A, **B** and **D** would all affect whether the calculation of the Glasgow train's arrival time is correct, but none are assumptions because all of these things have been stated in the passage. However, the passage has *not* stated that the trains will travel at the same speed, and if this is not true, then the conclusion that the Glasgow train will arrive at 8:30pm is no longer valid.

Question 58: A

C can actually be seen to be probably untrue, as the passage mentions a need to escape immune responses, suggesting that the immune system *can* tackle these cells. **E** is true but not representative of the main argument made in the passage. **B** and **D** are not *definitely* true. The passage mentions several *essential* steps that *must* occur, but this does not mean that they are *sufficient* for carcinogenesis to occur, or guaranteed to allow it. Equally, the passage makes no reference to multiple mechanisms by which carcinogenesis can occur. It could be there is only one pattern in which these steps can occur. **A**, however, can be reliably concluded, because the passage does mention several steps that are *essential* for carcinogenesis to occur.

Question 59: D

Answers **A** and **C** are stated in the passage (the passage states 'deservedly known'), so these can be reliably concluded. **B** can also be concluded, as it is stated that in over 50% of cancers, a loss of functional P53 is identified. **D** however, cannot be concluded, as the passage simply states that any cell that has a mutation in P53 *is at risk* of developing dangerous mutations. Thus, it cannot be concluded that a given cell *will* develop such a mutation.

Question 60: D

D is not an assumption because Sam's calculations are based on the *cost per 1000 miles*, not on a given amount of fuel being used up. Thus, he has *not* assumed anything about whether the fuel usage is the same for each car. All of the others are assumptions, which have not been considered. Each of these will affect the total saving he will make if they are not true. For example, if the Diesel car costs £100 more than the Petrol car, the total saving will be £1700, *not* £1800 as calculated.

Question 61: D

The passage discusses how alcohol is more dangerous than cannabis, and states that this highlights the gross inconsistencies in UK drugs policy. Thus, **D** is the main conclusion of the passage, whilst **A** is a reason given to support this conclusion. The passage simply highlights that the policy is grossly inconsistent, and does not mention whether it should be changed, or how (whether alcohol should be banned or cannabis allowed).

Thus, **B** and **C** are not valid conclusions from this passage. The fact alcohol is freely advertised only mentioned briefly in the passage to add strength to the argument that alcohol is more accessible than cannabis, but no judgment is made on whether this should not be so, so **E** is also not a valid conclusion from this passage.

Question 62: B

The passage discusses how if first aid supplies were available, many accidents could be avoided. B correctly points out that this is a flaw – first aid supplies may help treat accidents and reduce the prevalence of *injuries and deaths*, but there is no reason why first aid supplies should reduce the incidence of *accidents*. Answers **C** and **D** are irrelevant, since the argument is talking about how first aid supplies could reduce *accidents*, not *injuries* or deaths. Thus, discussing cases in which they could not treat the injuries, or whether they need other components to do so is irrelevant. Equally A is irrelevant, as the argument is simply talking about what could happen *if* first aid supplies were stocked in homes, and makes no reference to whether this is financially viable.

Question 63: C

Answers **A** and **D** are not flaws because the passage does not conclude the things mentioned in these. No mention is made to the safety of the drug, and the argument only states that it is thought the compound *may* be of use in combating cancer. No premature conclusions are drawn, only suggestions are made. **B** is not a flaw because we can see that the experiments *may* produce misleading results if the wrong solutions are used, suggesting that DNA replication is inhibited even if it is not. **C**, however, is a valid flaw because the argument erroneously concludes that the wrong solutions must have been used when it says the experiments *do not reflect what is actually happening*. This clearly indicates a conviction that the wrong solutions were used, which does not follow on from the experiments being old.

Question 64: B

The passage has not said anything about who scored the winning goal, so **A** is not an assumption. **C** is also incorrect, because the passage states that South Shields won the game. **B** correctly identifies that whilst beating South Shields was *sufficient* to win the league, it was *not* necessary. If Rotherham wins their other 2 games, they will still win the league, so **B** demonstrates an assumption in the passage. **D** is not relevant, as it does not affect the erroneous nature of the claim that Rotherham *will not* win the league having lost the match to South Shields.

Question 65: B

C and **D** actually strengthen or reinforce the CEO's reasoning, with **C** suggesting as time progresses Middlesbrough will have more and more people compared to Warrington, whilst **D** suggests that the market share in Warrington may not be as high as suggested, adding further reasons to build in Middlesbrough. **A** somewhat weakens the CEO's argument, but it is not a flaw in the reasoning, because the CEO is simply talking about how Middlesbrough will bring them within the range of more people, so the market share comment is a counterargument, not a flaw in his reasoning. **B**, however, is a valid flaw in this argument. Just because Warrington's population is falling, and Middlesbrough's is rising, does not necessarily mean that Middlesbrough's will be higher. Thus, the answer is **B**.

Question 66: D

1 and **2** are assumptions. The information given does *not* necessarily lead on to the conclusion that these extinction events will continue without further conservation efforts. Equally, there is nothing in the passage that says conservation efforts cannot be stepped up without increased funding. However, **3** is not an assumption, because the passage *states* that global warming has caused changed weather patterns, which have caused destruction of many habitats, which have led to many extinction events. Thus, it is given that global warming has indirectly caused these extinctions, and so the answer is **D**.

Question 67: E

The argument is suggesting that in Austria, the rail service's high passenger numbers and approval ratings are accounted for by the fact that road travel is difficult in much of Austria. It then concludes that the public subsidies have no effect. We can see that **I** instantly weakens this argument by providing evidence to the contrary, (in France, difficult road travel is not prevalent and so cannot account for the high passenger numbers/approval ratings the country possesses). **3** also weakens this conclusion by suggesting multiple factors affect the situation. This makes the conclusion based on the evidence from Austria less strong.

Thus, the answer is **E**. **2** actually strengthens the argument that the public subsidies do not cause high passenger numbers/approval ratings, as Italy has high subsidies but low passenger numbers/approval ratings.

Question 68: E

The question refers to companies selling a product despite being in full awareness of the problems that product is causing, and says that we should therefore tax this company to pay to tackle that problem. E) follows this reasoning. B) is the closest to this reasoning, but refers to individual patients paying for their own treatment, rather than referring to a company whose product is causing problems for others, and therefore paying for this damage. Meanwhile, A), C) and D) are not talking about those at fault for certain problems having to pay to fix that specific problem, and are therefore irrelevant.

Question 69: E

All of these statements cannot be concluded from the reference passage.

Question 70: D

Be careful of using your own knowledge here! Whilst **A** and **B** may be true, they are not the main message of the passage. **C** may be true but is not discussed in the passage. **E** is speculative, as the passage does not say if the transplant would be a 'good alternative'. **D** is correct as it echoes the main message of the passage.

Question 71: F

Smoking and Diabetes are risk factors for vascular disease (not a cause). Vascular disease does not always lead to infarction. The passage does not give sufficient detail about necrotic tissue to conclude **C** or **D**.

Question 72: B

A is irrelevant to the argument's conclusion. Meanwhile **E** does nothing to alter the conclusion, as the fact that schools receive similar funds does not affect the fact that more funding could provide better resources, and thus improve educational attainment. **C** actually weakens the argument; by implying that banning the richer from using the state school system would not raise many funds, as most do not use it anyway. **D** does not strengthen the conclusion as stating that a gap exists does not do anything to suggest that more funding will help close it. **B** clearly supports the conclusion that more funding, and better resources, would help close the gap in educational attainment.

Question 73: A

D and **E** are irrelevant to the argument's conclusion. **C** is actually contradicting the argument. **B** is stated in the passage, so is not an assumption of the passage. **A** describes an assumption: the increase of DVDs does not, necessarily, cause the loss of cinema customers.

Question 74: C

The question refers to aeroplanes being the fastest form of transport, and states that this means that travelling by air will allow John to arrive as soon as possible. **C** correctly points out that the argument has neglected to take into account other delays induced by travelling by aeroplane. Cost and legality are irrelevant to the question, so **B** and **E** are incorrect. Meanwhile, **D** actually reinforces the argument, and **A** refers to future possible developments that will not affect John's current journey.

Question 75: D

The argument states that people should not seek to prevent spiders from entering their homes. It does not say anything about whether people should like spiders being in their home, so **A** is incorrect. The argument also makes no allusion to the notion of people preventing flies from entering their homes, so **B** is incorrect. The argument also does not mention or implies that any efforts should be made to encourage spiders to enter homes, or that they should be cultivated, so **C** and **E** are also incorrect.

Question 76: A

A correctly identifies an assumption in the argument. At no point is it stated that bacterial infections in hospitals are resulting in deaths. **B**, **C**, **D** and **E** are all valid points but they do not affect the notion that pressure for more antibiotic research would save lives. Therefore, none of these statements affect the conclusion of the argument and as such they are not assumptions in this context.

Question 77: B

The passage does not state that John disregards arguments because of the gender of the speaker, so **D** is incorrect. **A** and **C** are also wrong, as John states he finds women with armpit hair necessarily unattractive, so a different face or the knowledge of concealed hair would not make him find the female in question more appealing to his aesthetic. John does not state Katherine wants other women to stop shaving, so **E** is incorrect.

B is the correct answer, as Katherine was simply speaking about societal norms, and at no point is it said she was trying to convince John to find her, with armpit hair, attractive.

Question 78: D

A is irrelevant to the argument, which says nothing about what will happen to Medicine in the future. The argument is describing how Sunita is incorrect, and how better medicine is not responsible for a high death rate from infectious disease in third world countries, and how better medicine will actually decrease this rate. **C** is a direct contradiction to this conclusion, so is incorrect. **E** is a fact stated in the argument to explain some of its reasoning, and is not a conclusion, therefore **E** is incorrect.

Both **B** and **D** are valid conclusions from the argument. However, **B** is not the main conclusion, because the fact that 'Better medicine is not responsible for a high death rate from infectious disease in third world countries' actually supports the statement in **D**, 'Better medicine will lead to a decrease in the death rate from infectious disease in third world countries'. Therefore, **B** is an example of an intermediate conclusion in this argument, which contributes to supporting the main conclusion, which is that given in D.

Question 79: A

The statement in A, that housing prices will be higher if demand for housing is higher, is not stated in this argument. However, it is implied to be true, and if it is not true, then the argument's conclusion is not valid from the reasoning given. Therefore **A** correctly identifies an assumption in the argument. The other statements do not affect how the reasons given in the argument lead to the conclusion of the argument, and are therefore not assumptions in the argument.

Question 80: B

A and **E** are both contradictory to the argument, which concludes that because of the new research, Jellicoe motors should hire a candidate with good team-working skills. **C** refers to an irrelevant scenario, as the argument is referring to only one candidate being hired, and at no point does it state or imply that several should be hired.

B correctly identifies the conclusion of the argument that Jellicoe motors should hire a new candidate with good team-working skills in order to boost their productivity and profits. **D** meanwhile exaggerates the consequences of not following this course of action. The argument does not make any reference to the notion that Jellicoe motors will struggle to be profitable if they do not hire a candidate with good team-working skills.

Question 81: E

D is in direct contradiction to the argument, so is not the main conclusion. Meanwhile, **B** is a reason stated in the argument to explain some of the situations described. It is not a conclusion, as it does not follow on from the reasons given in the argument. **A** and **E** are both valid conclusions from the argument. However, only **E** is the *main* conclusion. This is because both **A** goes on to support the statement in **E**. If bacterial resistance to current antibiotics could result in thousands of deaths, this supports the notion that the UK government must provide incentives for pharmaceutical firms to research new antibiotics if it does not wish to risk thousands of deaths.

Meanwhile, **C** appears to be another intermediate conclusion in the argument that also supports the main conclusion. However, on close inspection this is not the case. **C** refers to the UK government directly investing in new antibiotic research, whilst the argument refers to the government providing incentives for pharmaceutical firms to do so. Therefore, **C** is not a valid conclusion from the argument.

Question 82: B

E is completely irrelevant because the question is referring to an unsustainable solution *if* the UN's development targets are met, so the likelihood of them being met is irrelevant. **C** is irrelevant because they do not affect the fact that the situation would be unsustainable if everybody used the amount of water used by those in developed countries, as stated in the question. **A** is also irrelevant, as the passage does not mention price as a factor to be considered within the argument. Meanwhile, **D** would actually strengthen the argument's conclusion.

Therefore, the answer is **B**. **B** correctly identifies that if those in developed countries use less water, it may be possible for everyone to use the same amount as these people and still be in a sustainable situation.

Question 83: C

There is no mention of treatment, so **A** is incorrect. A need to travel abroad for the post is not stated either, so **B** is incorrect. The need for a cool head is stated explicitly, but not necessarily that this be a leader, so **D** is also wrong. Other qualities are irrelevant to the argument, so **E** is also incorrect. **C** would only be relevant if there was indeed a link between 'a specific phobia' and 'a general tendency to panic'. Thus, **C** highlights the flaw: if a fear of flying does not necessitate a general disposition of panic, the argument for not hiring this employee crumbles.

Question 84: C

The passage does not suggest there are no more university places, nor does it make a distinction between the qualities of different universities, so **A** is incorrect and **D** is irrelevant. The argument does not deny the fact that people can be successful without a university education, so **B** is also wrong. **C** is correct, as the passage specifically states 'many more graduates', but not all, are equipped with better skills and better earning potential. This suggests not all degrees produce these skill-sets in their graduates, and so not all university places will create high-earning employees.

Question 85: D

B is unrelated to the argument, as other contributing factors would not negate the damaging potential of TV. Watching sport on television would not be akin to actually playing sport, so **A** is also incorrect. The possibility of eye damage is stated as caused by TV, so **C** is incorrect. However, if people watch television *and* partake in sport, which the passage seems to imply cannot happen, they may not suffer the negative effects of obesity and social exclusion. For example, they may play sport during the day and watch television in the evening, thus experiencing the benefits of exercise and also enjoying the sedentary activity.

Therefore, various potential threats supposedly posed by watching excessive television are undermined, and **D** is correct.

Question 86: C

D directly counters the above argument, and so is incorrect. Though **A**, **B** and **D** are all suggested or stated by the passage, they each act as evidence for the main conclusion, **C**, describing the 'multiple reasons to legalise cannabis'.

Question 87: C

C is not an assumption as it has been explicitly stated in the question that the salary is fixed, and therefore it will not change. The rest of the statements are all assumptions that Mohan has made. At no point has it been stated that any of the other statements are true, but they are all required to be true for Mohan's reasoning to be correct. Therefore, they are all assumptions Mohan has made.

Question 88: A

The answer is not **B** because, although the Holocaust was a tragedy, this is not explicitly stated in the passage. It cannot be **C** or **E**, as these are also not directly stated above. **D** provides an intermediary conclusion that leads to the main conclusion of **A**: we should not let terrible things happen again, and through teaching we can achieve this, so therefore 'we should teach about the Holocaust in schools'.

Question 89: C

DVDs are irrelevant – though one could access disturbing material through a DVD, this does not mean the material to be seen on TV is less disturbing. The argument also is not concerned with adults, and the suggestion is that violence in any quantity may have a detrimental effect, even if a show is not entirely made up of it. **A, B** and **D** are thus not the correct answers. **C** contradicts the argument, as it suggests there is no link between witnessing and re-enacting what one has witnessed. Children may watch the scenes of rape and recognise the horror of the action, and so be sworn off ever committing that crime.

Question 90: C

A is irrelevant, as the passage states it *could* teach children, not that it necessarily would. **B** and **C** are also irrelevant, as the entertainment quality of the show or the likeability of its protagonist would not undermine the logic of the argument. **C** is the correct answer, as it shows how the question uses one model of success and projects it onto all other models, which is illogical: just because Frank succeeds without morality, does not mean all others must reject morality to succeed.

Question 91: A

B, C, D and **E** are all irrelevant to Freddy's argument that he cannot say a sexist thing because he is a feminist. The woman's discomfort, Neil's feminist stance, the appropriateness of making comments about men, or lewd comments in general do not affect his claim. The presumed link between the two (inability to say something sexist, and feminist self-description) is the flaw in Freddy's argument: someone may believe in equal rights for the genders, and still say a sexist thing.

Question 92: A

At no point is it stated or implied that car companies should prioritise profits over the environment, so C) is incorrect. Neither is it stated that the public do not care about helping the environment, so E) is incorrect. B) is a reason given in the argument, whilst D) is impossible if we accept the argument's reasons as true, so neither of these are conclusions.

Question 93: D

A) Incorrect. The text clearly states that the exercise routine is resistance training based.B) False. Both groups contain equal numbers of men and women per the text.

C) False. Both groups are age matched in the range of 20 to 25 years.

D) Correct. As the only difference between the two shakes is the protein content.

Question 94: B

B is the main conclusion of the argument. Options A and D both contribute reasons to support the main conclusion of the argument that the HPV vaccination should remain in schools. C is a counter argument, which is a reason given in opposition to the main conclusion. Option E represents a general principle behind the main argument.

Question 95: A

The main conclusion is option A that some works of modern art no longer constitute art. B is not an assumption made by the author as the main conclusion does not rely on all modern art being ugly to be valid. C is not an assumption because the argument does not rely on artists studying for decades to produce pieces of work that constitute art. This point is simply used to support the main argument. Options D and E are stated in the argument so are not assumptions. A is an assumption because it is required to be true to support the main conclusion but is not explicitly stated in the argument.

Question 96: A

Option B points out a flaw in the argument, which attributes the healthier circulatory system of vegetarians to diet, but ignores other potential contributory factors to a healthy circulatory system such as exercise. C is not an assumption: the health benefits of a vegetarian and omnivorous diet are not discussed; rather the argument is centred on the negative health ramifications. D is stated in the argument so is not an assumption and option E is a counter argument, not an assumption.

Option A is required to support the main conclusion but is not stated in the argument so is an assumption made in the argument.

Question 97: C
C- is the conclusion of the arguments presented. A is not argued in the text. B- is not the central conclusion. D- is stated as a belief only. E – is implied but not the conclusion.

Question 98: A
The passage argues that bottled water is pointless, as is almost identical to tap water. If bottled water had an additional benefit, such as being good for health, it might be that it makes sense to drink bottled water.

Question 99: C
A), B) D) and E) are all directly stated in the passage, so can all be reliably concluded. Perhaps the trickiest of these to see is answer D), which is true because the passage says "due to" the advent of more accurate technology, thus clearly identifying that this had caused the switch to the situation of most watches being made by machine. C), however, is not necessarily true. The passage states that most watches are produced by machines, but only states that some watchmakers now only perform repairs. This does not necessarily mean that most watchmakers do not produce watches. It could be that only a handful are required in the entirety of the watch industry for repairs, and that the numbers still producing watches exceeds those in the repair business. Thus, C) cannot be reliably concluded from the passage.

Question 100: A

B) is not a valid conclusion from the passage, because the fact that someone uses an illogical argument (as some pescatarians are claimed to in this passage) does not mean that they cannot use logic. D) and E) are not conclusions from this passage because the passage is not saying anything about the ethicality of eating meat, but simply commenting that one argument used against doing so is not logical. Answers C) and A) are both valid conclusions from the passage, but we see that if we accept C) as being true, it gives us good cause to believe that A) is true, but this does not apply the other way round. Thus, C) is an intermediation conclusion, whilst A) is the main conclusion.

FINAL ADVICE

Arrive well rested, well fed and well hydrated

The TSA is an intensive test, so make sure you're ready for it. You'll have to sit this at a fixed time (normally at 9AM). Thus, ensure you get a good night's sleep before the exam (there is little point cramming) and don't miss breakfast. If you're taking water into the exam then make sure you've been to the toilet before so you don't have to leave during the exam. Make sure you're well rested and fed in order to be at your best!

Move on

If you're struggling, move on. Every question has equal weighting and there is no negative marking. In the time it takes to answer on hard question, you could gain three times the marks by answering the easier ones. Be smart to score points- especially in section 2 where some questions are far easier than others.

Make Notes on your Essay

Oxford admission tutors may ask you questions on your TSA essay at the interview. Given that the interview will normally be 4 – 6 weeks after your TSA, it is essential that you make short notes on the essay title and your main arguments after the exam so that don't get caught off guard during the final hurdle.

Afterword

Remember that the route to a high score is your approach and practice. Don't fall into the trap that *"you can't prepare for the TSA"*– this couldn't be further from the truth. With knowledge of the test, time-saving techniques and plenty of practice you can dramatically boost your score.

Work hard, never give up and do yourself justice.

Good luck!

ACKNOWLEDGEMENTS

We would like to express our gratitude to the many people who helped make this book possible, especially the 10 TSA Tutors who shared their expertise in compiling the huge number of questions and answers. We are also grateful to the numerous editors who painstakingly provided valuable feedback throughout the authoring process.

ABOUT US

UniAdmissions currently publishes over 85 titles across a range of subject areas – covering specialised admissions tests, examination techniques, personal statement guides, plus everything else you need to improve your chances of getting on to competitive university courses such as medicine and law, as well as into universities such as Oxford and Cambridge.

This company was founded in 2013 by Dr Rohan Agarwal and Dr David Salt, both Cambridge medical graduates with several years of tutoring experience. Since then, every year, hundreds of applicants and schools work with us on our programmes. Through the programmes we offer, we deliver expert tuition, exclusive course places, online courses, best-selling textbooks and much more.

With a team of over 1,000 Oxbridge tutors and a proven track record, UniAdmissions have quickly become the UK's number one admissions company.

Visit and engage with us at:

Website (UniAdmissions): www.uniadmissions.co.uk

Facebook: www.facebook.com/uniadmissionsuk

YOUR FREE BOOK

Thanks for purchasing this Ultimate Book. Readers like you have the power to make or break a book —hopefully you found this one useful and informative. *UniAdmissions* would love to hear about your experiences with this book. As thanks for your time we'll send you another ebook from our Ultimate Guide series absolutely <u>FREE</u>!

How to Redeem Your Free Ebook

1) Find the book you have on your Amazon purchase history or your email receipt to help find the book on Amazon.

2) On the product page at the Customer Reviews area, click 'Write a customer review'. Write your review and post it! Copy the review page or take a screen shot of the review you have left.

3) Head over to www.uniadmissions.co.uk/free-book and select your chosen free ebook!

Your ebook will then be emailed to you – it's as simple as that!

Alternatively, you can buy all the titles at

www.uniadmissions.co.uk

MEDICINE PROGRAMME
Oxbridge

UNIADMISSIONS 2019 Oxbridge Medicine Programme Success Rate

The Average Oxford & Cambridge Medicine Success Rate

300+
Students successfully placed at Oxbridge in the last 3 years

50
Places available on our Oxbridge Medicine Programme in 2020

WHY DO OUR STUDENTS SEE SUCH HIGH SUCCESS RATES?

1 30 HOURS OF EXPERT TUITION.
UniAdmissions will guide you through a comprehensive, tried & tested syllabus that covers all aspects of the application - you are never alone.

2 UNPARALLED RESOURCES.
UniAdmissions' resources are the best available for your Admissions Test. You will get access to all of our resources, including the Online Academy, books and ongoing tutor support.

3 WEEKLY ENRICHMENT SEMINARS.
You'll get access to weekly enrichment seminars which will help you think like and become the ideal candidate that admissions tutors are looking for.

4 INTENSIVE COURSE PLACES.
By enrolling onto our Oxbridge Programme you will get reserved places for all of the Intensive Courses relevant to your application, such as the Oxbridge Interview Intensive Course.

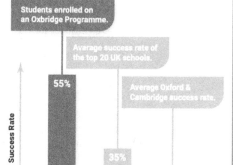

Students enrolled on an Oxbridge Programme.

Average success rate of the top 20 UK schools.

Average Oxford & Cambridge success rate.

Success Rate

55%

35%

13%

UNIADMISSIONS Oxbridge Medicine Programme Average Success Rate

Printed in Great Britain
by Amazon

27681354R10066